The Lost Salmon Flies of Balmoral

John Michie, 1853–1934
from a photograph by John Knight, Royal Studio, Newport, Isle of Wight

The Lost Salmon Flies of Balmoral

(Revised Second Edition)

COLIN INNES

With additional material by Dr Alison Innes
and
Flies tied by Edward Kublin

COCH-Y-BONDDU BOOKS
ANGLING MONOGRAPHS SERIES NO. 2
2018

The Lost Salmon Flies of Balmoral
First published as a limited edition 2015
Second revised edition 2018
produced in the
Coch-y-Bonddu Books Angling Monographs Series

© Coch-y-Bonddu Books Ltd 2018
Text © Colin Innes

ISBN 978 1 904784 88 3

Coch-y-Bonddu Books Ltd
Machynlleth, Powys, SY20 8DG
01654 702837
www.anglebooks.com

All rights reserved. No part of this may be reproduced, stored in a retrieval system, or transmitted, in any form or by any means, electronic, mechanical, photocopying, recording or otherwise, without the prior consent of the copyright holder.

*Dedicated to
Isabel, Ellie, Sandy and Mum*

Contents

PREFACE	9
ACKNOWLEDGEMENTS	12
CHAPTER 1 John Michie MVO (1853–1934), Factor at Balmoral *Written by Dr. Alison Innes*	15
CHAPTER 2 The Dee, Balmoral and its Fishing	19
CHAPTER 3 John Michie's Diary, fishing extracts 1885–1915	49
APPENDIX Lists of flies A comparison of beats on the River Dee, 1900–2015	105
BIBLIOGRAPHY	123

Preface

I had been aware for many years that I had a family connection to someone who had worked at Balmoral Castle, a Royal Family's holiday residence situated on the banks of the River Dee in Scotland, but I cannot say I had been very excited about it. There were some old photos in a dusty family album and access to twenty-three aged diaries written by our family connection, John Michie; not of much interest to me, I thought. That was until my mother started to document the diaries and mentioned fishing flies. That sparked some interest, and when she said, 'Oh, and I think it tells you what feathers he used,' well that was it, I had to know more. I had expected to see the familiar old patterns but soon realised that although these flies were similar in style to some of the recognised salmon fly patterns, they were not exact matches. They were flies that were tied to suit various conditions of a particular stretch of the River Dee flowing through the Balmoral Estate and had never been published or shared with the wider fishing community. Big flies, small flies, low-water flies, Eagles and Dee flies – in fact every fly you would need to fish the upper reaches of the Dee in the late 19th to early 20th centuries – with a commentary on when the flies were used and what they caught.

With my interest piqued, I started to read Mum's transcripts of the diaries, noting all the fishing passages, cross-referencing some of the famous names and researching some of the places, locating the pools on the three beats where John Michie had the right to fish. I started to like the modest man who was emerging through his commentary of daily life on the Queen's estate. The diaries are also a source of frustration; did he share his killing flies with the King, the Princes and the Princesses, the dignitaries of the day? And what did he think of them as fishermen? How did he feel on the 21st April 1911 when all he could write in his diary was the single line *"Mild weather. Had a cast in the evening & got 7 fish"*? What is the dressing of his 'Dragon' fly, mentioned more than once? Was it a mark of respect that on 13th March 1890 he went fishing on the Red Brae pool both before and after the funeral of an old gillie? One thing is for certain – John Michie was not happy at the end of February 1897 when he was falsely accused by the retired head gamekeeper, still living on the estate, of killing and selling the estate's salmon.

I suppose that John Michie's fly wallet has long gone so we will never know exactly what his flies looked like, but with the help of Edward Kublin I think we have at least a very good approximation of how they would have appeared. I first spoke with Eddie Kublin ten years ago when he contacted me to ask whether he could borrow a sample set of vintage Spey flies made by the Aberlour tackle company of J A J Munro at the start of the 1900s, as he wanted to photograph and study them. Unfortunately, three or four flies had been missing from the set, but when Eddie returned the set to me, the missing flies were no longer missing. Eddie had tied up replacements in the exact style of the originals; in fact, had it not been for a slight difference in the angle of the hook eye, you would not have been able to tell the old from the new.

Eddie had been educated at Seaford College in Sussex before joining the Royal Navy and serving on HMS Barrosa, a Battle-class destroyer that was part of the Mediterranean Fleet. He then attended the Royal Agricultural College in Cirencester and went on to farm in Suffolk, Devon and Aberdeenshire. While farming in Devon, he even built a trout fishery on his land. Eddie has been dressing salmon flies for over 36 years and has gained recognition as a 'Master Fly Dresser.' Now retired, he lives in Aberdeenshire and fishes the rivers Deveron and Spey, as well as the latter's tributary, the Avon.

Eddie has done a wonderful job of recreating the John Michie flies. He ties fishing flies in the old style, not as exaggerated exhibition flies, and they are all the better for it. I have no doubt that John Michie would have approved of them, and I am sure they would not have looked out of place in his own fly wallet; after all, Michie tied his own fishing flies for just himself, for catching fish in the River Dee. All of Eddie's flies that have been illustrated in this little book have been tied on antique hooks dating from the correct period and using the correct materials.

To help place John Michie's flies in the context of other flies that were being used on the River Dee at the time, I have provided patterns from contemporary sources and illustrations of period correct vintage flies from my own collection.

I hope that you enjoy this short excursion into the world of John Michie, life on the Balmoral estate at the end of the 19th and start of the 20th century and the flies that ensnared the noble Dee salmon.

Acknowledgements

I am greatly indebted to many people without whom this book would never have come to fruition. Here are a few of them:

- Alison Innes, my mother, who spent many hours typing and editing John Michie's 23 diaries. Mum, I hope this publication goes some way to making all your effort and research worthwhile.

- The late Joan Scudamore for allowing Mum access to John Michie's diaries.

- Carrie Walker for the epic and unenviable job of transforming my rambling, bad grammar and atrocious spelling into something that is readable.

- Martin Lanigan O'Keeffe (acknowledged as the world expert on the history of salmon flies) for many hours of discussion and debate on all aspects of the history of the salmon fly, for the original dressing of the Gordon and for helping to make this a more readable and interesting book. And also for giving my son, Sandy, the opportunity to catch his first Irish salmon.

- Anne Harper for her generosity in allowing me access to James Harper's records of his time as proprietor of the firm of William Brown of Aberdeen.

- Eddie Kublin for his tireless and incredibly fast work creating exceptional flies.

- Colin Simpson for supplying the original dressing of the Monaltrie.

- Philip Glendinning for being a fount of knowledge and information on both Dee flies and William Murdoch.

- Ryan Houston for giving me access to some wonderful information.

- Paul Morgan and his team at Coch-y-Bonddu books for turning a dream into a reality.

- The Flyfishers' Club for access to an (almost) complete run of the *Fishing Gazette* magazine.

And last, but not least, to Isabel, Ellie and Sandy for putting up with me spending so much time (and money) on my slightly obsessive interest in the old tackle and flies from Aberdeen.

John Michie and his wife Helen (née Kitchin), 1880s.
From a photograph by Milne of Blairgowrie

Chapter One

John Michie MVO (1853–1934) Factor at Balmoral

by Dr. Alison Innes

This book draws on the diaries of John Michie MVO (1853–1934), who was the Head Forester on Queen Victoria's Balmoral estate from 1880 until his appointment as Factor of the estate in 1901, a position he held until his retirement in 1919. His diaries record, among many other things, some of his salmon fishing experiences on the River Dee and the patterns of the flies that worked for him.

As Queen Victoria's Head Forester, John Michie was responsible not only for the management of the forests, but also for many other duties related to the running of the estate. Following the Queen's death in 1901, and the subsequent departure of Mr James Forbes, the Queen's Commissioner, to Blair Atholl, the new King Edward VII appointed John Michie to Forbes's post, changing the title from 'Commissioner' to 'Factor.'

As Factor, Michie had overall responsibility for the running of the estate, and like many other of the men employed at Balmoral, he was a member of the 'Balmoral Clansmen' or 'Balmoral Highlanders,' eventually becoming their leader. These Highlanders were equipped with uniforms (highland dress), and had the duty of escorting important visitors from the gates of Balmoral to the castle, often bearing torches. One such occasion was in October 1896 when the Tsar and Tsarina of Russia and their baby daughter, the Grand Duchess Olga, visited Balmoral. John's wife Helen was invited to the Castle to see the baby, and the Tsar presented John with a platinum cigarette case studded with diamonds and sapphires.

On Queen Victoria's death in January 1901, John Michie and three other Balmoral Highlanders travelled to Osborne House on the Isle of Wight, where she had died, and accompanied the Queen's coffin to Cowes, from where it was taken by yacht to Portsmouth. They subsequently escorted the coffin from Windsor railway station to St George's Chapel at Windsor Castle for her funeral service. The Balmoral Highlanders also paraded at the annual Braemar Gathering. It was the custom of large Scottish estates to have such contingents, which were, in effect, private armies, and the tradition still survives in the form of the Lonach Highlanders.

John Michie's diaries document the happenings on the estate, recording and describing with clarity the usually everyday but sometimes momentous events associated with the comings and goings of the Royal Household, and the tasks involved in the routine management of the estate and its personnel. There are records of his own life with his wife and seven children, living first in the Danzig Shiel, then Abergeldie Mains (on his appointment as Factor) and, from 1904, in Bhaile-na-Choille, which continues to this day to be the residence of the current Factor at Balmoral.

John Michie's factual diary entries are often elaborate, with personal comments and opinions – always respectful when making reference to his royal employers, but not so guarded when dealing with those with whom he worked. A not infrequent entry was "then the Queen came to tea…". He made astute observations on world events and local, national and international personalities. He gave a graphic account of life as lived by a Victorian family on a Scottish estate in the latter part of the 19th century and through the years of the 1914–18 World War, when his four sons were serving officers in the British Army.

Twenty-three of John Michie's diaries survived in the safe keeping of the Michies' daughter Alix (Alexandrina) who married Colonel John Milne and lived in an old manse in Ballater where the Muick meets the river Dee. Alix and John had three daughters, and one of them, Joan (who married Joe Scudamore), kindly made the diaries available to me. Joan and Joe were both medics and emigrated to

Australia where they had three children; Ian, Duncan and Kirstin, who have inherited and retained ownership of the house in Glen Muick – and the diaries. In addition to the surviving diaries, a considerable amount of relevant material, including a 'John Michie Box,' can be found in the Royal Archives in the Library at Windsor Castle.

In the following chapters, abbreviated, but not edited, extracts from the diaries are printed verbatim with the original punctuation and spelling.

Of course, there is no suggestion in John Michie's writings that he had any notion that they would be used by his great niece Alison and her son Colin as a source of material for publication more than one hundred years later.

Figure 2.1 Current beat map of the River Dee

CHAPTER TWO

The Dee, Balmoral and its Fishing

The River Dee rises high in the Cairngorm mountains and travels 90 miles to exit into the North Sea at Scotland's third largest city, Aberdeen. Along its course, it passes the villages of Braemar, Crathie, Ballater, Dinnet, Aboyne, Kincardine O'Neil, Banchory, Drumoak, Culter, Milltimber, Bieldside and Cults (Figure 2.1), although the last four of these would now be considered suburbs of Aberdeen. The Dee is the sixth largest river in Scotland, draining an area of around 800 square miles and falling about 4,000 feet from its source to the sea. It has two major sources, both springs, one near the summit of Ben MacDhui (a mountain with an altitude of 4,296 feet) and the other from Braeriach (a mountain with an altitude of 4,252 feet). The river runs through every aspect of Scottish terrain, starting with mountains, progressing through hills and forests, and continuing on to the relatively flat areas around Aberdeen. Perhaps the most beautiful parts of the river are found from Braemar down to Aboyne.

The River Dee is a perfect river for flyfishing for salmon. There are no major obstructions in the river and very little pollution, allowing the salmon a clear run up to their spawning grounds. The upper river is fast, streamy and not very deep (averaging about 4 feet), runs over granite shingle and is generally very clear. Along the banks are woods of birch, fir and pine, with hills of heather and rowan trees. The middle reaches lose none of the water's momentum and twists and turns between the pools. The water starts to slow a little below Banchory, providing excellent spring fishing. There is a spring run of salmon, a summer run of grilse and sea-trout, and an autumn or 'back-end' run of salmon. Unlike the River Tay or Tweed, the Dee is not known as a river for large fish. Although there are of course exceptions to this rule. The average fish weighs in at around the nine pounds mark.

The Dee's main tributaries are as follows: above Braemar, the Lui Water and the Quoich Water; at Braemar, the Clunie; at Crathie, the Gelder Burn and the Girnock Burn; and just before Ballater, the River Gairn and the Muick. At Aboyne, there are the Water of Tanar, the Burn of Birse and the Tarland Burn, and just before Banchory can be found the Burns of Cattie and Canny. In Banchory, there is the Water of Feugh. The Sheeoch Burn comes in at Kirkton of Durris, and finally in Culter there is the Culter Burn.

Scottish salmon rivers are usually split into 'beats' or lengths of river that are individually owned (although there are exceptions where a whole river system can be owned by one individual). A beat can be a single side of a river, both sides or a combination of some 'single-bank' and some 'double-bank' stretches (the convention for identifying the sides of a river generally refers to the 'right' or 'left' bank when looking downstream). Fishing rights would have originally gone with the land and been under the control of the owners of the country estates the river ran though. Over time, however, this has changed, and some of the estates have since sold off their fishing rights.

In the late 19th century, the beat owners would either have kept the fishing for themselves, their friends and families or let the fishing for the whole or a part of the season. Nowadays, most beats are generally let by the week, with the tenant being given the option to rent the same beat for the same week the following year. Currently, due to demand, if you have a prime beat at a prime time on the Dee and do not renew your lease, it will be snapped up by someone on the waiting list and you may have lost it forever.

The beats of the River Dee today number just fewer than 70. These have not changed much since John Michie's time, and in the Appendix I have included a table comparing the beats in 1900 with the current ones. This chart also details the proprietors who were listed in 1900.

In 1872, the Marquis of Huntly (of Aboyne Castle) and Sir William Cunliffe Brooks (the owner of Glen Tanar) formed the Dee *Salmon Fishing* Improvement Association to improve the rod fishing on the Dee (and hence the value of the beats) by removing the netting of salmon below Banchory. There were 16 netting stations between Banchory and the Bridge of Dee, and the Association set about buying the net fishing rights. In the first 10 years, it spent around £4,000, resulting in a cessation of netting from Banchory down to the railway bridge in Aberdeen. This action was a great success, and the rentable value of rod fishing significantly increased. John Michie was proposed to the Association's committee by Sir Cunliffe Brooks, joining it in 1903. The Association is still active today.

When Queen Victoria first visited the Highlands in 1842, she promptly fell head over heels in love with the countryside. After a subsequent visit to Scotland, she decided that a holiday home was required and leased the Balmoral estate unseen. Victoria took possession of the 'pretty little castle' in 1848 and was so pleased with it she started negotiations to buy the lease. The purchase of the estate from the Trustees of Mar was completed in 1852, when she became the outright owner. Immediately, and with the help of a £250,000 legacy, plans were made to build a castle that was more suitable for a royal holiday residence. Situated closer to the river, the new castle was completed in 1856, at which point the old castle was demolished, the royal party having used this while the new building was being constructed.

Balmoral remained Victoria's 'dear Paradise' for the rest of her life and was passed to King Edward VII on her death. During her time at Balmoral, Victoria built cairns, obelisks, monuments, fountains, wells, suspension bridges, roads and cottage-type retreats (called shiels) all over the estate. Victoria loved its wilderness and wildness. She was always out and about on the tracks and trails of the estate, shunning the day-to-day concerns of state and the castle to find her own space where she could just be herself. The shiels provided her with stopping-off points where she could take tea, paint, breathe the mountain air or just relax and watch the deer.

It seems, however, that the royal family was not satisfied with the amount of land and housing on the Balmoral estate, and soon set about adding to it. Close to the east of Balmoral is the 16th-century Abergeldie Castle (Abergeldie meaning 'confluence of the clear stream'), which was (and still is) owned by the Gordon family. The Queen approached the Gordons with the aim of buying Abergeldie, but they did not want to sell the property, which had, after all, been in their family for over 400 years. They did, however, agree in 1848 to lease it to Queen Victoria. The land came with six miles of fishing rights on the south bank of the Dee, which joined with the bottom end of the Balmoral beat. The castle also came with a resident ghost called 'French Kate.'

The demand for quality housing for the Royal family and guests was still not yet satisfied, so the next year saw the first purchase of Birkhall (which means 'birch river meadow'), another large country house and its land. The owners were again the Gordons of Abergeldie, who this time agreed to an outright sale. With this addition to the royal property portfolio came yet another two miles of the River Dee. Once the freehold of Balmoral was established, the Queen gave Birkhall to the Prince of Wales, and then in 1884 bought it back from him.

A few miles to the south-west of Balmoral is Ballochbuie forest, 2,500 acres of Caledonian pine forest including trees of up to 400 years old. The forest is home to a wide range of wildlife including deer, capercaillie and the now extremely rare Scottish crossbill. In 1878, when the owners, the Farquharsons of Invercauld, planned to sell the trees to an Aberdeen timber merchant, Queen Victoria stepped in to buy the forest in what is thought to be the first act of forestry conservation.

Towards the end of the 19th century, the Balmoral beat was referred to as 'Balmoral & Ballochbuie' and was recorded as being six miles long. Adding this beat to the rented Abergeldie water and the owned Birkhall water, John Michie had access to 14 miles of prime upper Dee fishing on the south bank and an additional seven miles of the north bank at Crathie which Victoria was leasing from Mr

Farquharson. Birkhall now belongs to Price Charles who inherited it from the Queen Mother on her death in 2002. It is clear from his diary that Michie had leave to fish whenever the water was not being fished by the Royal family or their guests. He also seems to have fished in the mornings and evenings. In those days, it was usual for an estate with fishing to have what they termed 'fishermen', usually made up of outdoor workers such as gardeners, foresters, gillies, etc. They were allowed to fish, but all the fish caught would be given to the estate for consumption or selling.

As already mentioned, the Dee is a perfect river for flyfishing, and today it is the only way that the river is fished. However, that was not always the case. Fish were seen as something to be harvested for the table or sent to Aberdeen to be sold to the highest bidder. Major James Dickie, in *Forty Years of Trout and Salmon Fishing* (1921), tells us about his fishing holidays on the Queen's waters. On a trip in June 1920 while fishing the Douchels pool with Lundy, one of the Balmoral gillies, he writes: "I put up a prawn and killed a fish of nine pounds. Then one of six and a half pounds," and later in the day:

> In the lower part of the [Newton] pool where there was no run to carry the fly, I saw quite a lot of fish rise, and although I did try a fly over them, it wouldn't fish properly owing to the lack of stream. I put on a prawn and killed four fish of seven and a half pounds, eight pounds, seven pounds and six and a half pounds.

In my copy of Dickie's book, a contemporary reader has written next to the text, "I saw the blighter! Started to prawn just in front of me with a fly. Blast him!" The same reader also pencilled in at the start of the chapter: "Poor old Lundy hated the prawn, which we never used and apologised profusely to us for Dickie's use of it!" Lundy seems to have the same attitude to prawn fishing as Michie, as can be seen from his diary entry for Friday 9th May 1890: "Walked to Dr. Profeit's who gave me some prawns & asked me to try for a fish as he had to go to Strathdon to see a horse. Killed a fish in evening not with prawn which I detest to fish."

The best description I have found of Mr Dickie was in the *Aberdeen Press and Journal* newspaper under the title 'Angling guest of a king' on 29th April 1942:

> Aberdeen Rotarians heard fishing stories yesterday from a man who was once a guest of the late King George V for several angling holidays. He is Major J L Dickie, who as a surgeon did splendid work for wounded in the last war. Some of his achievements were in caring for badly wounded men at the Star and Garter Home in London. The late King George was among the many famous people who visited the centre. Seeing Major Dickie's rod standing in a corner, he asked about his angling and learned that the Dee was one of the Major's favourite haunts. Soon afterward came a message from the king inviting him to spend his leave on the Balmoral, Abergeldie, and Birkhall waters and saying that accommodation had been arranged for him at a farmhouse. For his fishing reminiscences Major Dickie drew from rich experience. He began fishing for minnows in Aberdeen's Denburn and since then has ranged the banks of many well-known rivers in Scotland and England, fished for Himalayan trout in India, and once caught dolphin from the deck of a liner in the Indian Ocean. Mr WP Humphreys presided, and Mr James Harper thanked the speaker.

To fully understand the flies that Michie documents in his diary, we need to have some knowledge of the flies in general use by the salmon fishers on the Dee during the late 19th and early 20th centuries. Salmon flies have different 'styles', and the flies used in this period can be broadly split into the following five categories:

- general flies that could be found in use on any river in the UK and other countries where *Salmo salar* swims;
- fancy flies that were specifically designed for the Dee;
- plain strip wing Dee flies that were used primarily (but not exclusively) in the springtime;
- simple summer or low-water flies designed for the River Dee;
- the outrageous Eagle flies.

The fly patterns that John Michie used and documented in his diaries include flies from four of these categories: general flies, Dee strip wings, summer or low-water flies and Eagles. Although these bear similarities to existing standard patterns, some are unique and, perhaps more importantly, they caught fish on the Balmoral fishing beats.

To establish the flies that were commonly used on the River Dee at the end of the 19th century and start of the 20th century, I have referred to the 1897 catalogue from the firm of William Brown, which, along with William Garden and Charles Playfair, was one of the most important tackle-makers in Aberdeen. This firm, which had a long history, was acknowledged by most of the respected contemporary authors of fishing books, including Francis Francis (in the 1860s), George M Kelson, Francis Walbran and T E Pryce-Tannatt (in the early 20th century). In the 1897 catalogue, there is a long list of salmon flies, over 560 salmon patterns and also a special list of 41 standard salmon flies for the River Dee.

We are lucky that Dee flies had a champion in William Murdoch, who documented the patterns, ways to fish them and when to fish them in a series of articles during the 1880s in the weekly periodical the *Fishing Gazette*. I base most of my definitions of the Dee-specific flies on this source and have supplemented them with further detail from books and catalogues published during the period. In 1884, Murdoch conducted a most useful survey of the most popular Dee strip wings and Eagle flies in use on the Dee; the results of the survey, along with Brown's 1897 list of Dee flies, are given in the Appendix, and many of these flies are similar to the ones that John Michie records in his diary.

William Murdoch was born in 1853 (coincidently the same year at John Michie) and died in 1925. The following obituary was published in the *Aberdeen Press and Journal* newspaper on 30th November 1925 which gives a good account of his life; it is worth noting that the position of chief teller was one of the highest ranked positions at the bank, so he would have retired a relatively wealthy man:

A well known personality on Deeside has been removed by the death of Mr William Murdoch retired bank teller, who passed away yesterday at his residence, Logie Mar, Banchory, at the age of 74. Mr Murdoch who was an authority on natural history subjects connected with birds and animals of all kinds was a recognised authority on the life and haunts of salmon, more particularly on the River Dee, which he knew as an angler from its mouth to its source. Only recently he published a book, entitled *More Light on the Salmon*, in which he described "what a Dee salmon sees, hears and does on its journey from the grey north sea to the mountain pool in the Cairngorms," being a series of articles which he had contributed to the *Fishing News*. Mr Murdoch was also a frequent contributor to the *Aberdeen Press and Journal*, and the *Scottish Field*.

The article's writer is not aware of Murdoch's significant contributions to the *Fishing Gazette* in the 1880s, or that Murdoch patterns were also quoted in some of the earlier Hardy catalogues and contemporary books such as Kelson's *The Salmon Fly*, Walbran's *British Angler* and Hale's *How to Tie Salmon Flies*. The obituary continues:

A native of New Deer, Mr Murdoch on leaving School, entered the services of the North of Scotland Bank, in which he remained for over 40 years. He was in the head office of the bank at Aberdeen for over 30 years, and he occupied the position there of chief teller when he retired and went to live at Banchory ten years ago. With plenty of leisure time at his residence on Deeside Mr Murdoch had ample opportunity to indulge his love of angling and his study of salmon life and of the other branches of natural history in which he was so profoundly interested. He became one of the most familiar of Dee anglers, and won the friendship and confidence of the Deeside gillies, and he had a wonderful knowledge and a fund of anecdote and story gleaned from conversations with old gillies of the river Dee which he put to good use in the numerous lectures which he delivered from time to time up and down Deeside and in other places. In addition to the study of animals and fish Mr Murdoch was a keen botanist, and latterly took up gardening, devoting himself to floriculture with as much enthusiasm as he had bestowed on the natural history subjects. Everything he went into he did thoroughly and mastered, so that he was regarded as one entitled to speak authoritatively on the fauna and flora of Deeside.

It was from this enthusiasm there was born the idea of the Deeside Field Club, which he mooted to kindred spirits and he was fortunate in enlisting the interest and support of the Marquis of Aberdeen and Temair, and it is to the Marquis, and more particularly Mr Murdoch himself, that the inception and success of the Deeside Field Club are due. It was founded in June, 1920, and with Mr Murdoch as its indefatigable and enterprising secretary it met with immediate success and had a remarkably original membership, almost wholly due to Mr Murdoch's efforts. He was particularly successful in securing for its membership most of the Deeside landed proprietors whose active sympathy was a great stimulating factor. This club from its very start has been one of the most successful of its kind in Scotland. After two years' devoted service to the club Mr Murdoch resigned on account of ill health, and was appointed an honorary vice-president in appreciation of his services to the club.

Well versed in such topics as have been indicated, and with a keen desire to impart his knowledge to others, Mr Murdoch was a most interesting companion to meet and have a walk and talk with, and he was a most racy and entertaining lecturer and writer. His house at Banchory was a great place of call with persons interested in the subjects on which Mr Murdoch could speak with so much authority. Mr Murdoch who was unmarried took no part in the ordinary public life of Banchory devoting himself entirely to his studies and hobbies.

As previously mentioned Murdoch published a little book entitled *More Light on the Salmon: What a Salmon sees, hears and does on its journey from the Grey North Sea to the mountain pool in the Cairngorms*, which tells the tale of a salmon as it migrates up the River Dee, describing the beats and the flies that were used to tempt him. Although the book lists salmon flies used on the Dee, it does not contain any fly dressings. Murdoch died not long after his book was published and four days after his 74th birthday in November 1925.

The following paragraphs expand on the categories of flies used in the rest of my book.

Figure 2.2 General flies – From left vintage Childers, Popham and Jock Scott

General flies

During the 19th century, salmon flies went from the fairly basic, drab flies of the late 18th century to wondrous flies created from all sorts of exotic feathers. There are several reasons why this happened.

First, due to the Victorian craze for adorning ladies' hats with feathers, there was an influx of exotic feathers from all over the British Empire. Fishermen, and particularly fishing tackle-makers, were quick to pick up on this new material and added brightness and colour to their salmon flies. After all, it has always been easier to lure a fisherman than a salmon!

Secondly, a number of important books were published around the middle of the 19th century which contained both descriptions and illustrations of gaudy salmon flies, allowing fly-tiers to emulate them. These included Blacker's *Art of Angling* (several editions from 1842 to 1855), *Jones's Guide to Norway* by Frederic Tolfrey (1848), Wade's *Halcyon* (1861) and Francis Francis's *A Book on Angling* (six editions from 1867 to 1886).

In addition, at the start of the 19th century, out of necessity, the majority of salmon anglers fished their local rivers, and it was only the very rich who could afford the cost and time taken to fish further afield. During the rest of the century, travelling became much easier, cheaper and, most importantly, quicker. This gave ordinary mortals the chance to fish in far-flung rivers. Then Queen Victoria bought the Balmoral estate on the banks of the Aberdeenshire Dee and made the fishing holiday in Scotland very fashionable. With this new mobility, salmon fishers became exposed to new rivers, fishing methods and new styles of flies.

Finally, by the end of the century, Kelson had published his monumental work *The Salmon Fly* (1895), which had been many years in preparation and was largely based on articles he had written in the 1880s for the *Fishing Gazette* and *Land & Water*, and which followed Hale's *How to Tie Salmon Flies* (1892). Thus, the fully-dressed fly was established in every angler's fly wallet. No self-respecting salmon fisher would be without a Jock Scott, Childers or perhaps even the very exotic Popham (Figure 2.2). The popularity of the fully-dressed fly continued into the early 20th century, with further important books on the subject being published. These included the complex flies described by Pryce-Tannatt in *How to Dress Salmon Flies* (1914), and the more pragmatic contributions of Eric Taverner's *Salmon Fishing* in the Lonsdale Library series, 1931.

The fad for the fully-dressed fly started to wane after the Second World War, when exotic feathers became more difficult to obtain and a new breed of fishermen started to appear who took a more scientific approach to salmon fly design and developed flies using simpler, more easily available materials.

This category of general flies also includes flies other than the fully-dressed fly, for example grubs, strip wings and low-water flies, the important point being that they were not specifically designed for use on the River Dee.

Figure 2.3 Fancy Dee flies – From the left vintage Gordon, Mar Lodge and Sherbrooke

Fancy Dee flies

Fancy Dee flies are similar to general fully-dressed flies in that they have complicated bodies and multi-part wings. However, they were designed specifically for use on the River Dee. They are often dressed on long shank Dee hooks similar to the Dee strip wing flies. In many cases, these flies were very successful fishing flies and went on to catch fish in many other locations, both at home and abroad.

The best known pattern of this style of fly is perhaps the Gordon (Figure 2.3 and 2.4). This was designed by Cosmo Gordon, the earliest written description and dressing details (located so far) being published in *Land & Water* magazine on 5th February 1870. The article was attributed to 'A Forester' and described a fishing trip to the Dee in April 1869:

> On my first day I made but a poor hand of it, as I used Mr. Brown's flies, but on the second, after an evening's chat and a comparison

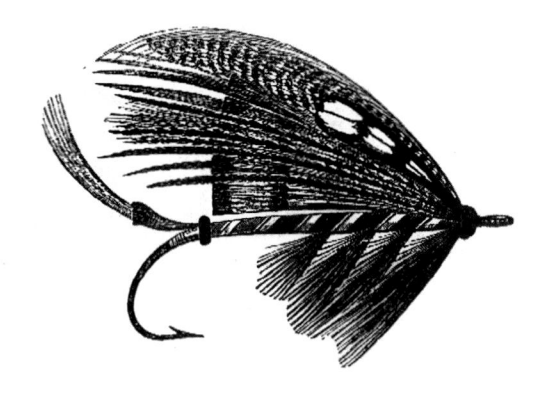

Figure 2.4 The Gordon

of notes with my two friends who were located there with me, my bag told a different tale. For this good sport I am purely indebted to Mr. Cosmo Gordon, a gentleman whose exploits with the rod must deservedly class him amongst the foremost rank of salmon fishers. The dull brown wings, and the fluffy looking eagle bodied flies, were soon transferred to that omnium gatherum pocket of my book where all such waste tackle goes to, in case they might be useful upon an occasion, and in their place I used flies twice their size, dressed upon Phillips' hooks and of gaudier colours. These were purely the invention of Mr. Gordon and tied by us both.

Murdoch also includes the pattern in an article in the *Fishing Gazette* in 1884 and notes:

The best fly of the fancy order put upon the River Dee, the Gordon, dressed sparely, and on slender wire, cuts the swiftly flowing water most beautifully, and plays immense havoc amongst the fish. In spring and autumn no fly approaches it for general usefulness, or is half so much used. A veteran and a favourite, the Gordon has never lost an inch of ground. The best fly for coloured or high running waters, it competes with the Grey Eagle for the first place as an evening lure; in short, it is better known on the Dee than any other fly.

The Gordon has many variations. Kelson, for example, lists two versions in *The Salmon Fly* (1895), one each from the Aberdeen

Figure 2.5 The Mar Lodge with Her Royal Highness the Duchess of Fife and presumably John Lamont on gaffing duties.

tackle-makers William Brown and William Garden. I have listed the original pattern from *Land & Water* in 1869 and Murdoch's patterns in the next chapter. The illustration in Figure 2.4 is from the *Fishing Gazette*.

Other examples of flies in this category include the Mar Lodge (Figure 2.3, 2.5 and A.5) and the Sherbrooke (Figure 2.3).

The 'Mar Lodge' was named after an estate on the upper reaches of the River Dee. Kelson attributes this fly to John Lamont: 'John Lamont hit on a grand idea at the time when he invented this pattern and forwarded a specimen to Garden of Aberdeen to introduce it to his Deeside customers'; 'Her Royal Highness the Duchess of Fife was most successful with the pattern.'

The present Mar Lodge was completed in 1898 for the Earl of Fife and his wife, Queen Victoria's granddaughter Princess Louise (Princess Royal and the Duchess of Fife). The house is famous for its ballroom, with around 2,500 stag heads attached to the ceiling. The person responsible for arranging and conserving the heads was taxidermist and gillie John Lamont. John lived in a cottage on the estate next to a pool on the River Dee quaintly known as 'Stuffer's Pool.' It is strange that some of the more recent compilers of salmon fly patterns incorrectly refer to John Lamon rather than Lamont (this may be because of a printer's error in *The Salmon Fly*, however Kelson's *Land & Water* cards are correct).

Further information about the Mar Lodge has come to light recently. Newspaper sources from around 1900 suggest that the Duchess of Fife designed the pattern herself, which I doubt. Perhaps the most interesting theory has come from Martin Lanigan-O'Keeffe in his recently published book *Farlows Salmon Flies*, from which I quote the following:

> This fly needs no further comment, except to note that the pattern was designed in 1889, as a 'nondescript,' by William Brown, the Aberdeen tackle-maker, for Henry Gordon of Manar (on the river Don). The intention was to produce a black and white fly, and in its original dressing the wing has no dyed swan, but did have various

brown strands as well as tippets from a cross between Amherst and golden pheasants, which nearly always turned out black and white. This last, which was not generally available, was in time substituted by summer duck. The fly was obviously discovered to be useful on the Dee, was copied, given a more colourful wing, and in the course of its transit acquired its present name. David Bell, who had become the proprietor of William Brown after the death of its founder [*this is not quite correct as JW Laing owned the firm after the death of Brown before Bell took over – for further details of the history of the firm see* The Salmon flies of James Harper *written by the author*], had originally intended to call the fly the Manar, but by the time examples with the fancier wing were brought into him to copy it had become known as a Mar Lodge.

The Sherbrooke is described by Kelson in *The Salmon Fly* as 'a great favourite at Braemar.' Kelson attributes this fly to William Garden of Aberdeen; I have not managed to confirm that this is the case and assume that, as usual, he means that he got the pattern details from William Garden. I have used the same spelling, 'Sherbrooke,' as the firm of William Brown does in both its 1897 and 1902 lists. Kelson, Pryce-Tannatt, Hale, Hardy, Garden and Playfair, however, use the spelling 'Sherbrook.'

MARCH, 1890.

Thursday, 20. To workmen at new walk Craig-gowan. About half is now totally completed but the most difficult piece to manage is yet to go over, viz, that immediately above the East entrance. Weather extremely detrimental to working in the ground. In the forepart there was constant drizzling rain which after noon turned into dry snow covering the surface at dusk to the depth of 3 inches or so.

Went to Garlin with the fishing rod at 5 o'ck and at 6 killed a fish of 8tts below the big stone. Hook- Gold Pheasant tip, yellow and green body. Silver tinsel/broad, eagle + teal hackle, turkey wing of light soiled red with black bar and white tips put on these sizes of hook 2½ inches long.

Saw two Ayrshire cows which came to Invergelder this week.

Friday, 21. At home making out Monthly accounts and Paysheets. Sent David McEwan to Dr Profeits with accounts. Helen heard from a Cousin Sam Stephen Walker who is at College at Aberdeen to the effect that he intends coming to spend a few days at Danzig when the session ends on the 26th inst.

This morning the ground was white with soft snow which had melted by noon and again by mid afternoon the weather got quite mild. Fished from 6 to 7 but no rises.

There is to be a rifle shooting at Broughdhu, Birkhall tomorrow but I do not incline to go.

Saturday, 22. Sawmill and ordered fencing to be ready for walk Craig-gowan on Monday. Mrs Stewarts wood, (near School House Crathie) to be ready on Wednesday. Marked 14 trees on Garralt hillock as well as 8 below to go to Mill. Dr Profeit arrived home from Windsor yesterday. Paid workmen at Balmoral and Danzig.

Fished in evening with ordinary sized water and medium sized flies round by bridge of Dee without a rize. Put on the large hook described below, and killed two fish with it- one in pool under wooden bridge the other being in pool of Gold P¹ crest tip. Oval silver tinsel along with broad flat. Body blue spot of lace then yellow, green, blue in equal quantity. Heron grey roll hackle, hackle jay. Wings- spotted turkey with black tips, 3½ inches long. full size hook. 3 inches exactly xx

An example page from John's diary

Figure 2.6 Typical vintage Dee strip wing flies – From the top: Killer, Glentanar, Killer with gold tinsel and four colour body, Tartan and Tricolour.

Dee strip wing flies

This is the style of fly that is usually referred to as a 'Dee fly' (Figure 2.6). A typical Dee strip wing could be described as follows:

Tag: Silver tinsel.
Tail: Golden pheasant tippet, topping or saddle feather (or a combination of them).
Body: Single or multiple colour sections of mohair, pig's wool or seal's fur.
Hackle: Black or grey heron breast feather tied through the body.
Throat: Teal or other wildfowl flank feather.
Wing: Two strips of turkey tail feather, tied so that they lie flat and horizontally over the body spreading away from the head, originally the tail feathers of the red kite (known locally as the Gled) were used.
Cheeks: Where called for are jungle cock nail feathers tied so that they droop down from the head
Hook: Long shank Dee hook.

In 1885, William Murdoch gives the *Fishing Gazette* reader the following hints for a perfect Dee strip wing fly:

> For spring patterns the conventional long shanked Dee irons – a special manufacture of Bartleet and Sons, Redditch – are all but universally used: that is to say, so long as the weather is cold, and the volume of water somewhat more than ordinary in size. For spring patterns, the irons range from 1¾ inches to 4 inches in length, and the Limerick bend is the approved style. The wings, which are strips of turkey feather, should be placed on the upper part of the shank at the head so as to naturally extend about 10 degrees outward at the tips after being tied. In length, except when toppings are used, they ought to stretch quite to the tip of the tail, or somewhat further than the extremities of the bend, the precise length that symmetry may be

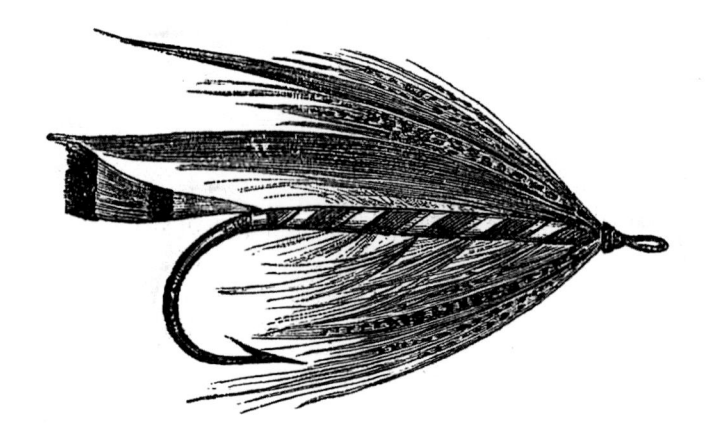

Figure 2.7 A Gled Wing

shown, to be determined by the size of the iron. The correct length of the tail feather or fibres should be likewise so regulated. When hackles of black or grey heron are used, they ought to be of the longest fibre, and wound on sparely and spirally down to the point indicated in the descriptions.

The illustration of a Gled Wing (one of the earliest Dee patterns) from the *Fishing Gazette* in 1884 (Figure 2.7) demonstrates how a correctly tied Dee strip wing should look.

The above description holds good for most of the early Dee flies. There are of course variations, for example the Moonshine (Figure A.4 and A.5), in which the first half of the body from the tail is formed from silver tinsel and has a peacock butt both at the tail and centrally in the body, with veils of exotic chatterer or kingfisher. However, the Dee-style strip wing always remains the same.

Henry Wade, in *Halcyon*, published in 1861, goes so far as to suggest a general Dee pattern: 'Wings, mottled turkey's feather, either brown or white; body dark mohair, heron hackle, silver tinsel; shoulders, a twitch of yellow or orange mohair; tail tuft yellow.' This dressing is a fairly close match to the Dee flies at the end of the 1880s. The earliest recorded Dee fly is the Tartan.

Tartan

The Tartan (see Figure 2.6) is a very old pattern. The first recorded version that I know of appeared in *The Driffield Angler* by Alexander Mackintosh in 1806; although not quite the same as the patterns of the late 19th century, it is similar. The Tartan was also recorded in *Halcyon* by Henry Wade in 1861, *By Lake and River* by Francis Francis in 1864, and *A Book on Angling*, also by Francis Francis, in 1867. The Francis Francis pattern of 1867 gives an excellent description of how the Tartan is tied and what it should look like:

Tag: Gold tinsel.
Tail: Gold pheasant rump.
Body: Half orange and half scarlet-red mohair laid on sparely, of course; broadish gold tinsel also spare.
Hackle: First a stripped sandy-red cock's hackle (that is, only one side of it to be used, the other being stripped off), and on top of this, the large blue-grey hackle or feather from the heron's back and rump; the larger the better, they cannot be too large, as when the hackle is laid on, the fibres are expected to extend from the very head to the farthest bend of the hook. It is an awkward feather to lay on, as are all heron hackles, being very delicate. It should be tied in, to commence from as low down as it can be conveniently tied so as to leave enough for a good thick brush from the head. If in winding on the hackle, any of the red hackle fibres under it be wound in, they must be picked out afterwards with the needle, and put in their proper position. At the shoulder, a teal hackle of course.
Wings: Two strips of silver-grey mottled turkey (the small mottled feather); these feathers are not easy to get.

When the fly is finished, and before it is properly pressed down into shape, it looks like an enormous spider, or daddy longlegs; it certainly is a monstrosity, though, after all, not such a monstrosity as the Eagle. The Tartan is a strange looking fly and is rather a troublesome fly to dress. From Mr. Brown's Dee patterns.

Murdoch gives us his version of the Tartan in the *Fishing Gazette* on the 23rd February 1884:

Tag: Silver tinsel.
Tail: Red cock feather.
Body: One turn orange, two turns blue, and three turns claret mohair.
Ribbing: Silver tinsel, broad.
Hackle: Grey heron (sparingly) down body.
Shoulder: Teal.
Wing: Distinctly marked black and white turkey.
Head: Black.

On 8th March of the same year, he follows this up with a quite different pattern:

Tag: Silver tinsel.
Tail: Golden pheasant, saddle feather.
Body: Either orange and scarlet mohair in equal proportion, or two turns orange, two turns scarlet, and two turns blue mohair.
Ribbing: Gold tinsel.
Hackle: Grey heron, partly down body.
Shoulder: Teal.
Wings: Mottled turkey of brownish shade.
Head: Black.

Dee strip wing flies tend to fall into two sub-groups: flies that have black heron hackles, and flies that have grey hackle feathers. There is huge scope for variation, with different body colours, different tail feathers and differently coloured turkey wings. Every gillie on the Dee and every fly-tier in Aberdeen, Ballater, Aboyne, Kincardine O'Neil and Banchory would have had their own pet versions. I think that the Tricolour and the Glentanar are the perfect 'model' or 'standard' flies that the others (with a few exceptions, such as the Akroyd and Moonshine) are based on – and one could argue that the Tricolour is based on the Tartan, and the Glentanar on the Gled or Red Wing.

Tricolour

The Tricolour (see Figure 2.6 and A.5) is one of the most common Dee flies after the Akroyd (Figure 3.12, A.1 and A.5). I do not believe that Murdoch presented the dressing for the Tricolour to the *Fishing Gazette*, but luckily the *British Angler* by Walbran (1889) contains a dressing for it that he attributes to Murdoch:

Tag:	Silver thread.
Tail:	Golden pheasant's red rump feather.
Body:	A couple of turns each of yellow, light blue, and turkey red mohair (well picked out).
Ribbed:	Broad silver tinsel and silver twist.
Hackle:	Long grey heron's (dressed full), with teal at shoulder, and also between the wings.
Wings:	Either white, sandy, or cream colour, according to fancy.
Head:	Varnished.

It is worth noting a couple of things about the Tricolour.

First, if you add a red golden pheasant rump feather instead of teal at the shoulder, you end up with a fly known as the Killer (see Figure 2.5 and A.1). The Killer was responsible for Mrs Clementina 'Tiny' Morison's British record fly-caught salmon of 61 pounds from the River Deveron on 21st October 1924.

Secondly, in my collection I have quite a few Tricolours and Killers, and I can confirm that there are many variations in the body colour, number of colours (generally three, but not uncommonly four) and the order of those colours. In my experience, the most common body has yellow at the tail end, red in the middle and pale blue at the head, which is unlike the sequence given in the patterns recorded by Murdoch, Kelson, Hardy and Pryce-Tannatt.

Glentanar

There are as many dressings of the Glentanar (see Figure 2.6, A.1 and A.5) as there are ways of spelling its name. It is named after the Glen Tanar estate on the banks of the Dee above the village of Aboyne. The estate in turn takes its name from the glen through which the stream called the Tanar runs. The Tanar joins the River Dee on the Craigendinnie beat at a pool called Tanar Mouth, just above the Lorne pool. These can be fished from either the Aboyne Castle beat (north or left bank) or the Craigendinnie beat (south or right bank) – a place I have fished for over 14 years. The dressing quoted below was the first to be published by Murdoch and appeared in the *Fishing Gazette* on 23rd February 1884.

Tag: Gold tinsel.
Tail: Fibres of golden pheasant tippet.
Body: Orange-red and blue mohair in equal proportion – blue at head; red in the centre and yellow beside tag. Orange in body well picked out.
Ribbing: Gold tinsel and silver twist.
Hackle: Black heron.
Shoulder: Teal.
Wing: Red turkey.
Head: Black.

Murdoch must have done some more research, or perhaps someone challenged the pattern, as the Glentanar next appears in the *Fishing Gazette* on 8th March of the same year. In his description, he states:

We have to secure unanimity of opinion on the dressing of the 'Glentanar.' There seems to be two patterns, almost identical – in fact, since the difference is so trifling that they may be regarded as one and the same. But a third pattern, said to be as good as if not better killer than either is also put forward. We therefore consider it necessary to give a detailed description of these patterns, notwithstanding the fact that a preponderance of evidence favours the idea that No. 1 is the correct and original 'Glentanar' fly.

Numbers I and II are indeed nearly identical, differing only in shade of body material. Version III, however, seems to be almost a Tricolour with a black heron hackle.

Glentanar I

Tag: Silver tinsel.
Tail: Golden pheasant rump feather.
Body: Two turns dark orange and two turns dark brown mohair. [Version II replaces brown mohair with claret mohair]
Ribbing: Silver tinsel and gold twist.
Hackle: Black heron.
Shoulder: Teal.
Wings: Brown turkey.
Head: Black.

Glentanar III

Tag: Silver tinsel.
Tail: Golden pheasant rump feather.
Body: Yellow, blue and orange mohair in equal proportions, mohair of the body well picked out.
Ribbing: Silver tinsel.
Hackle: Long black heron.
Shoulder: Guinea fowl.
Wings: Brown turkey, gradually inclining to a lighter shade towards the tips.
Head: Black.

Summer or low-water Dee flies

Of all the five styles of fly discussed here, it is the summer or low-water flies (Figure 2.8) which are still in general use today. The larger flies have all been replaced with modern alternatives. Only a few enthusiasts fish with them. However, these smaller, less heavily dressed flies are still actively fished in the summer or in bright weather conditions, with great success. In general, they are much simpler than the full dress flies, and as a result they are a cheaper option for the fisherman. They often comprise a simple body, a single throat hackle and a wing of mallard or teal flank feather. Some are designed to give the impression of a fully-dressed fly, but simpler and smaller; for example, the Jeannie (Figure 2.8) impersonates the Jock Scott, and the Logie (Figure 2.8) does the same for the Gordon.

Although they are simpler and smaller flies, don't be fooled: a good low-water fly needs real skill to dress well. They tend to be tied on a lighter 'low-water hook' or 'wee double', and they fish higher up in the water. They were very suited to the 'greased line' method of fishing popularised and extensively written about by Donald Rudd under the pseudonym 'Jock Scott' in his books *Greased Line Fishing for Salmon* (1935) and *Fine and Far Off* (1952). Readers interested in this style of fly should read the little gem of a book *Salmon Fishing: The Greased Line on Dee, Don and Earn*, written by Frederick Hill, one-time gillie at the Carlogie beat of the River Dee (between Aboyne and Banchory), in 1948.

Some of the best known low-water flies include the aforementioned Jeannie and Logie, as well as other classics such as the Blue Charm (Figure 2.8) and Silver Blue (Figure 2.8). It is hard to believe that Murdoch supplied the dressing for the Blue Charm in 1884. Today, most anglers would perhaps associate it with A H E Wood, owner of the Cairnton beat of the River Dee, who popularised it in the early part of the 20th century.

(Opposite) Figure 2.8 A box of vintage summer or low-water flies, top row; Silver Blue and March Brown, second row; Logie, Jockie and another version of the Logie, third row; Blue Charm and Jeanie, fourth row; more of the above.

45

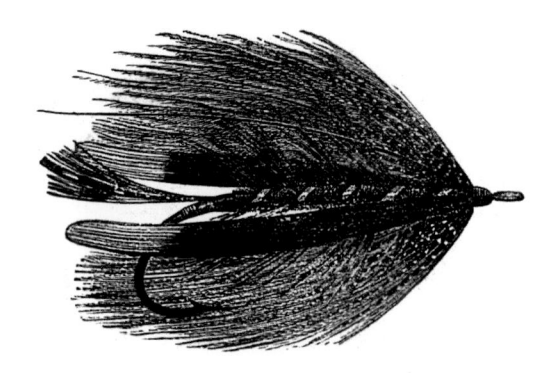

Figure 2.9 White Eagle

Eagles

The Eagle flies are always of interest as they are quite unlike any other type of salmon fly. They are basically a Dee strip wing fly, but instead of the usual Heron hackle, they utilise the fluffy feathers (called 'fluffies') found on the thigh of an eagle. It is perhaps shocking in our modern world, but during the 19th century it was quite usual for gamekeepers to shoot eagles as vermin. This resulted in a ready supply of fluffies, and, of course, the enterprising salmon fly dresser took advantage of them to create unique flies with very mobile hackles. Eagles tend to be tied on rather large long shank Dee hooks. Figure 2.9 shows a White Eagle from the *Fishing Gazette* in 1884.

In this chapter I have attempted to paint a picture of the environment and the typical salmon flies in use on the River Dee during the years John Michie lived and worked on the Balmoral estate. I hope that this will help you to understand and enjoy his commentary in the next chapter.

Figure 2.10 A selection of vintage Eagles

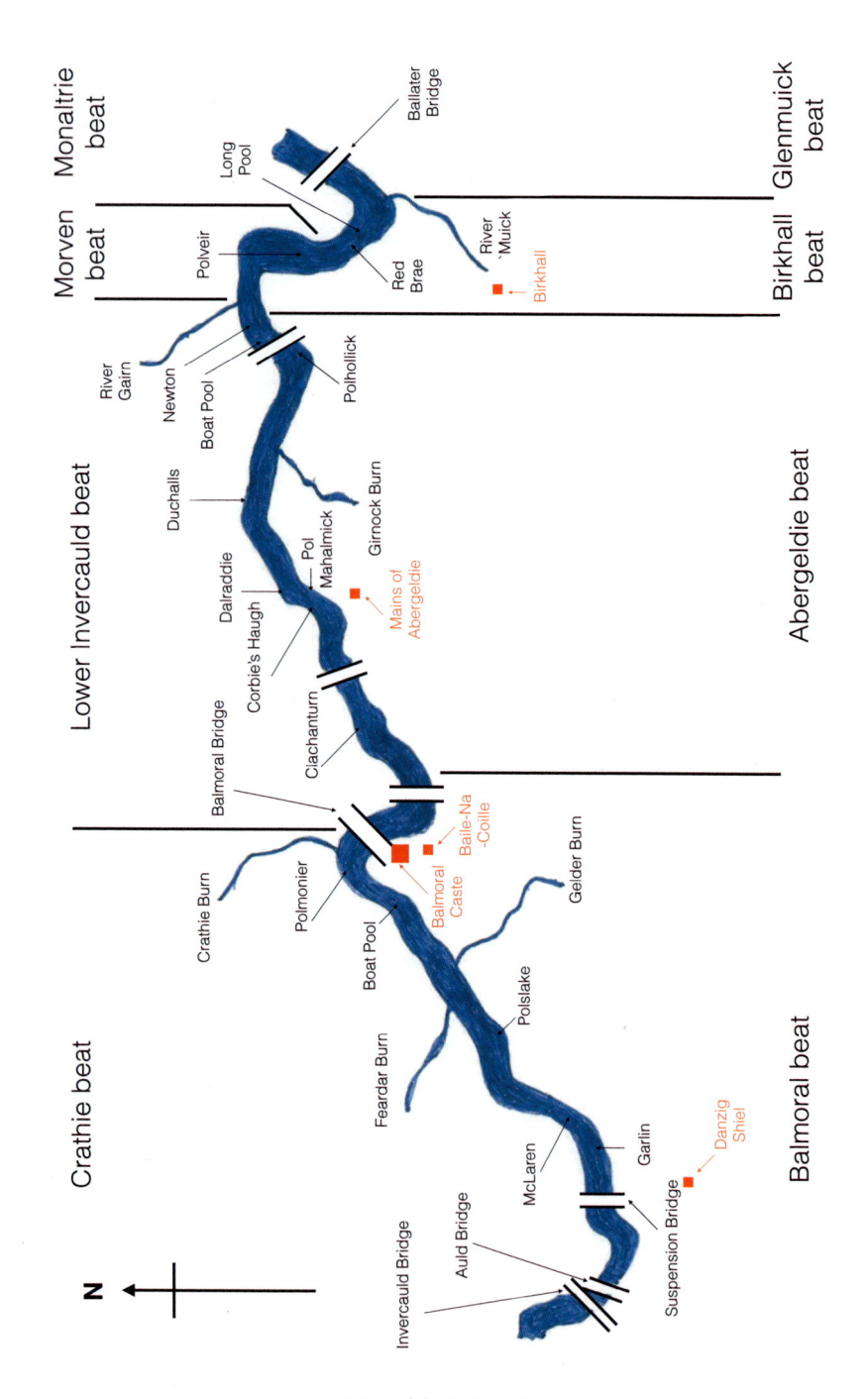

Figure 3.1 Map of the Balmoral estate beats

48

CHAPTER THREE

Fishing extracts from John Michie's Diaries 1885–1915

The following are unedited diary extracts in italics, with a commentary from the author. The salmon pools that John Michie mentions in these extracts are indicated on the map in Figure 3.1; also highlighted are the houses on the Balmoral estate where John and his family lived.

1885

Thursday 5 February: Remained at home all day doing some odds & ends. In the afternoon did some writing and dressed a few flies in view of the approaching fishing season which commences on the 11th instant.

Augustus Grimble, in his definitive work of 1899–1900 *The Salmon Rivers of Scotland*, writes, 'The Dee is fished with every description of lure: flies, prawns, natural minnows, gudgeons, and artificial spinning baits of all sorts are freely used.' From this entry and subsequent diary entries, it is clear that John Michie intends to fish the more gentlemanly fly at all times.

Friday 10 April: A very wet day. Went to fish with Dr Profeit & Dr Anderson. The latter caught 2 salmon with a little fly of mine. I hooked one in the evening with an identical hook but lost him after a long run.

Dr Alexander Profeit was the Commissioner at Balmoral for twenty years where he had overall responsibility for running the estate. He died in 1897. Scott Skinner (a well known Scottish composer) wrote a Strathspey called "Dr Profeit" in his honour. A Strathspey is a graceful complex Scottish dance (4 beats in a bar) and is usually much slower than a Scottish Reel (2 beats in a bar) which is fast moving and danced in "sets."

After Dr Profeit died his position passed to James Forbes.

1890

Tuesday 25 February: Remained at Ballochbuie [Forest, the location of John's house, Danzig Shiel; Figure 3.2] all day. At sawmill & Glen Beg in forenoon, afterwards dressed 3 salmon flies, and fished but got no rises. Weather fine very cold & frosty wind from the east.

In Scots, 'shiel' means roughly made hut or shelter; Danzig Shiel was built by the Queen in 1882 and named after a sawmill operator from the German town of Danzig. With anti-German feelings running high during the First World War, the house was renamed Garbh

Figure 3.2 Danzig Shiel – John Michie's first house on the Balmoral estate

alt Shiel after the nearby picturesque Falls of Garbh Allt. It was one of Queen Victoria's favourite picnic spots; 'Rough made hut' it is certainly not!

> ***Thursday 27 February***: *Dressed some salmon flies and attempted a cast but the line would not pass the rod rings on account of the severe frost.*

The freezing of the line to rods and rings is still a common problem today. One way of rectifying it is to dip the rod into the water for a few seconds between every cast.

> ***Friday 28 February***: *On arrival home at 2 o'clock landed a salmon of 10 lbs the first I have got this season. It took a small fly – gold pheasant tail (crest). Black floss silk body with small show of orange at root of tail, silver tinsel, black cock's hackle, with teal at head and wild drake wing. Iron of hook 1 3/8 long. This is the smallest hook I ever fished with at this season yet the fish took it in preference to larger & more elaborately dressed fly. The river was small & clear.*

A Small Fly

This fly (pictured overleaf, Figure 3.3) would fit into the category of summer or low-water flies, unusually small to be fishing with in the early spring, but as John Michie says, 'the river was small and clear.' The fly is quite similar to the Clunie (Figure 3.9).

Tail: Gold pheasant (crest).
Body: Black floss silk body with small show of orange at root of tail.
Rib: Silver tinsel.
Hackle: Black cock hackle, with teal at head.
Wing: Wild drake. [The bronze coloured flank feather of a mallard drake]
Hook: Iron of hook 1 3/8" long [equivalent to a size 1 1/2]

Figure 3.3 Top: 'A Small Fly'. Bottom: 'A Favourite Small Hook'. Tied by Eddie Kublin

The Clunie

In a *Fishing Gazette* article about grilse flies for the Dee in 1884, Murdoch states that the Clunie:

> has this year been used with much success in the upper reaches of the Dee, and in this stream from which its name is derived, especially as a salmon pattern, it has attained great popularity from Ballater upwards. To appearance it seems a likely grilse pattern. This fly was shown to us by William Garden of Aberdeen.

The Clunie (Figure 3.9) has also been referred to as the Clunie Snail, which is an apt description, the Clunie's teal wings are tied in a 'tented' fashion, giving the distinct impression of the shell of a snail. There are two other versions of the Clunie: The Brown Clunie illustrated in William Garden's catalogue of 1917, and the Grey Clunie, mentioned as being used with success on the Birkhall beat of the Dee during 1916 by Dickie in *Forty Years of Trout and Salmon Fishing*. The Clunie is still used today; it is very effective in the upper beats of the River Dee, especially during the summer months of the season:

Tag: Silver twist.
Tail: A small topping.
Butt: One turn black herl.
Body: Black silk floss.
Ribbed: Silver tinsel, 5 turns.
Wings: Double strips, distinctly marked teal.
Hackle: Guinea fowl, only at shoulder.
Limericks, 6 and 7, double irons.

Other similar teal or mallard wing flies used on the Dee include the Jeannie, Logie, Sailor the Blue and Green Charms. We will look at the last two charming flies later on, but following here are Murdoch's patterns for the first three.

Jeannie

In a *Fishing Gazette* article about grilse flies on 21st June 1884, Murdoch introduces the Jeannie (Figure 2.8) :

> It is a popular salmon fly in the early summer. Hitherto, it has been used most generally about Aboyne, Ballater, and Braemar. It is nothing more nor less than an inexpensive substitute for a Jock Scott (Figure 2.2). We have not yet used it for grilse, but reckon it would take fairly well. It may be regarded as a good general fly, the size to be used being regulated by the state of the water.

Murdoch also states that 'We have failed to trace the originator of this fly.' Kelson attributes the pattern to William Brown, and as usual the fly pattern compilers follow.

The Jeannie is still used today as a low-water fly, both in its traditional form and as a hair wing:

Tag: Gold twist.
Tail: Small topping.
Body: Black and orange silk floss, two-thirds black, one third orange, orange nearest to tag.
Ribbing: Gold flat worm.
Hackle: Black only at shoulder.
Wings: Double strips of very dark mallard – i.e. four pieces, two at each side, the one above the other. With or without a topping over wing.
Cheeks: Jungle fowl.
Head: Black.
Double Limericks – sizes, No. 4, 5, and 6.

We will take a look at the Jock Scott later in this chapter.

Sailor

When Murdoch listed the Sailor in an 1886 edition of *Fishing Gazette*, he raved that:

> in so far as harmonious blending of colours is concerned, the Sailor is inferior to no fly ever invented. A tempting and smart looking fly, it has a very pretty appearance in the water. For a change from the ordinary run of flies, a better could not be desired. On the Dee it has this season proved, and is still proving, very deadly; while on several rivers to the north it is working wonders. No fly tied by Mr. Garden, Fishing Tackle Maker, 122½ Union Street, Aberdeen, is so much sought after at present. The sizes between No. 3 and No. 7 are the best. Pretty much a summer, or rather, small water fly, the Sailor cannot be dressed large, the wing being nothing but four strips of teal.

Tag: Silver twist.
Tail: A topping
Body: Equal sections of bright yellow and light blue fur.
Ribbed: Oval silver tinsel.
Hackle: Greenish blue over the light blue fur.
Wing: Double strips of finely marked teal, on either side; topping over.
Cheeks: Chatterer.
Head: Black wool.

Logie

In the *Fishing Gazette* of 9th August 1884, Murdoch states that the Logie (Figure 2.8) :

> is virtually a plain 'Gordon,' as the body is almost identically the same. This fly stands unrivalled in the Aboyne and Ballater districts during the latter half April and the month of May, if the water is anywise small. As no fly can approach the 'Gordon' for

general use from Banchory to Ballater, so this small representation of it occupies during the period we have stated, a like unique position.

Murdoch also describes this pattern as 'an old Dee pattern'. In his delightful little book *Salmon Fishing: The Greased Line on Dee, Don and Earn* (1948) Frederick Hill lists two versions of the Logie: one for March that is similar to Murdoch's version (although the body is equal halves yellow and red, with silver round tinsel and the hackle greeny blue), and one for April, again similar but this time the body is silver tip, remainder red silk, and ribbed with silver oval or embossed tinsel and a blue hackle. The Logie is still used today as a low-water fly, both in its traditional form and as a hair wing:

Tag: Silver thread.
Tail: Small topping.
Body: Yellow silk floss one third, claret silk floss to head for the rest. The yellows to be the same shade as yellow swan.
Hackle: Blue, only round shoulder.
Wings: Yellow swan under; mallard strips over.
Head: Black

Limericks, sizes 6, 7, and 8, used for salmon and grilse.

As Murdoch compares this fly with 'a virtually plain Gordon,' and as the Gordon is probably one of the most famous Dee fancy flies, it is probably worth pausing and giving it some thought.

The Gordon

As previously mentioned, the first recorded pattern of the Gordon (Figure 2.3 and 2.4) was published iwn the *Land & Water* magazine in 1870:

Tail: Red & blue macaw.
Butt: Black ostrich.
Body: A few turns yellow, then claret floss.
Rib: Silver twist.
Hackle: Blood red all the way.
Wing: Mixed.
Hook: Large.

Although this reads as a very different pattern to later versions, when it is tied up the overall effect is very similar. It is worth mentioning that Cosmo Gordon also used blue jay in the shoulder hackle. Murdoch published the dressing details for the Gordon in the *Fishing Gazette* twice – the first, as below, on 16th February 1884:

Tag: Silver tinsel and yellow floss.
Tail: A topping and fibres of golden pheasant tippet.
Butt: Black ostrich herl.
Body: One turn orange, three turns claret floss.
Rib: Silver tinsel and gold flatworm.
Hackle: Claret.
Shoulder: Light blue cock hackle.
Wing: Under wing, two large golden pheasant tippets on either side, fibres of teal and bustard, golden pheasant tail, blue, red, and yellow swan. Topping over all.
Cheeks: Jungle cock.
Horns: Blue macaw.
Head: Black.

Two years later, Murdoch published a more complex and deluxe version:

Tag: Silver thread and orange [medium] floss. [yellow floss changed to orange]
Tail: A topping and Indian crow. [Indian crow replacing the more utilitarian tippet]
Butt: Black ostrich.
Body: Four turns orange [medium] floss, the remainder claret colour floss, medium shade.
Ribbed: Silver tinsel and silver twist. [silver twist replacing gold flat worm]
Hackle: Claret, to match body, from orange floss.
Throat: Greenish-blue hackle.
Wing: Two tippets back to back extending to butt, with a rump feather [red] projecting about ½in.; bustard, pheasants tail, peacock wing, dark brown mallard, blue, red and yellow swan, and a considerable quantity of bronze herl; topping all over. [adding golden pheasant rump feather, peacock wing, mallard and bronze herl]
Sides: Jungle. [two spots]
Horns: Blue macaw.
Head: Black wool.

Friday 7 March: *Fished in the evening but caught no fish had a salmon "on" for a few seconds with a small fly at Big Stane* [a pool on the Balmoral beat of the Dee], *Brig O'Dee – a March Brown was the allurer although the river was above ordinary size, but it was clear. Rain fell heavily the whole afternoon which changed to snow at dusk.*

March Brown

The March Brown (Figure 2.8) is a standard fly. It can be used as a trout fly, a low-water or summer fly or occasionally in a larger size for the spring (I have seen a vintage March Brown tied in Dee strip wing style on a long shank Dee hook of length equivalent to a 9/0 hook). The earliest pattern I have found for it as a salmon fly is in Kelson's 1895 book *The Salmon Fly*; here he describes it as an 'old standard on the Dee' and 'dressed on small double hooks.' Kelson's pattern has a fairly exotic body of monkey's fur, and I think that Michie would probably have gone for the more common and simpler body of hare's ear:

Tag:	Gold twist.
Tail:	A topping.
Body:	Silver monkey's fur and a little dirty-orange seal's fur, mixed together.
Ribs:	Gold tinsel (oval).
Throat:	Partridge hackle.
Wings:	Hen pheasant tail.

Thursday 13 March: *Went to the funeral of William Stewart who was at Balmoral in the late Prince Consort's time as a gillie. He wrought under me until about 5 years ago when he had paralytic stroke since which he has been unable to work. William in religion was a Roman Catholic. The Revd. Mr Paul of Braemar performed the funeral service. Caught a salmon in the morning & hooked & lost 2 in the evening – all in the Red Brae pool. Weather mild but blowing a hurricane still.*

Saturday 15 March: *Weather – strong wind from south with showers of rain, later continuous rain. Fished in evening but caught nothing except a wet skin.*

I remember that feeling well – God bless Gore-Tex!

Thursday 20 March: *Went to Garlin* [a pool on the Balmoral beat of the Dee – I have also seen it spelt Garlinn and Garlum] *with the fishing rod at 5 o'clock and at 6 killed a fish of 8 lbs below the big stone – hook – gold pheasant tip, yellow and green body, silver tinsel (broad), eagle & teal hackle, turkey wing of light soiled red with black bar & white tips put on thus:*

size of hook 2½ inches long.'

The Garlin

The Garlin (Figure 3.4) is a typical Eagle type fly used on the Dee (see examples in Figure 2.9), but although similar to known patterns it is not the same as any published pattern:

Tail:	Gold pheasant tippet.
Body:	Yellow and green body.
Rib:	Silver tinsel (broad).
Hackle:	Eagle & teal hackle.
Wing:	Turkey of light soiled red with black bar & white tips put on as per sketch above.
Hook:	2½ inches [roughly equivalent to the length of 7/0 hook].

Figure 3.4 The Garlin tied by Eddie Kublin

There is only one other Eagle fly that has green in the body, Maxwell's White Eagle, which can be found in his 1898 book *Salmon and Sea Trout*.

Maxwell's White Eagle

- *Tag*: Silver tinsel.
- *Tail*: A topping and tippet sprigs.
- *Body*: In three equal divisions. yellow, green and yellow pig's wool.
- *Rib*: Broadest silver tinsel.
- *Hackle*: Eagle hackle un-dyed, of a silvery tone, pintail hackle at shoulder
- *Wings*: Long strips of grey turkey with black bars.
- *Head*: Very small, black varnish.

Eagles

There are many different Eagle patterns (Figure 3.9), each tackle-maker and fly tier having their own variations. However, Murdoch's Dee fly survey in 1884 (see the Appendix for details of the survey and patterns) identified the three most popular Eagle flies in use on the Dee as the Yellow Eagle, Grey Eagle and White Eagle; Murdoch also gave directions on which fly to use in different prevailing fishing conditions:

> The black bodied "Grey Eagle" answers its purpose best on a cloudless evening after sundown, when brought to play upon clear, streamy water with a gravelly bottom. In the evening, when the sky is unclouded, a "Yellow Eagle" is decidedly the best pattern to use in fishing deep pools. When a nebulous condition of atmosphere exists, fortune seldom favours abundantly. At such times, however, we cannot do better than recommend a trial of the "White Eagle" for pool or stream after sunset.

Francis Francis gave a very graphic description of the Eagle flies in his 1867 *A Book on Angling*, in the section 'Mr. Brown's patterns':

> Some of the flies used [on the River Dee], as the Eagle (local 'aigle;' and here I may say that the Aberdeenshire dialect is the worst and most non-understandable to a stranger of any in Scotland; for, though tolerably experienced, I never could understand half my gillie said when they were conversationally inclined during my visits there) – I say the 'aigle' is little more marvellous as a fly than the dialect is as a dialect, and if we might liken some flies to shrimps and prawns, and others to butterflies and dragon flies, the Eagle completely knocks all such possibilities on the head, as it is like nothing on, over, or under the earth.
>
> The Eagle – There are two Eagles, the grey and the yellow. The yellow is simply the same feather as the grey, only dyed a bright canary yellow; indeed, I believe, in the evening, the 'yellow aigle' is the favourite, and is the more effective fly of the two.
>
> The tail, body, &c., are precisely similar to those of the gled wing; a quantity of the down or fluffy part of the golden eagle's feather – the

part on and above the leg is, I fancy, the best – is then wound on like a hackle, till the fly looks like the butt end of a largish eagle's feather itself; on the shoulder is of course the invariable teal hackle; wings, two broadish strips of silver grey turkey; the large mottled or broad striped and banded feather being selected.

Murdoch's Eagles

The following three Eagle patterns appeared in an article in the *Fishing Gazette* on 23rd February 1884. The Grey Eagle is an unusual one in that it has a black body rather than the usual two- or three-colour body of most Eagle flies.

Grey Eagle

Tag:	Silver tinsel.
Tail:	Golden pheasant rump feather.
Body:	Black mohair well picked out.
Ribbing:	Broad silver tinsel.
Hackle:	Grey eagle.
Shoulder:	Teal.
Wing:	Mottled turkey wing, brownish tinge.
Head:	Black.

White Eagle

Tag:	Silver tinsel.
Tail:	Golden pheasant rump feather.
Body:	Red and blue mohair in equal proportions – blue nearest head.
Ribbing:	Silver tinsel, broad.
Hackle:	White eagle down – a considerable quantity.
Shoulder:	Teal.
Wings:	Black and white turkey.
Head:	Black head.

Yellow Eagle

The Yellow Eagle is perhaps the most common of the Eagle fly family. Murdoch listed two patterns of the Yellow Eagle, the first on 23rd February 1884:

> *Tag*: Silver tinsel.
> *Tail*: Golden pheasant rump feather.
> *Body*: Two turns blue mohair, and two turns claret mohair.
> *Ribbed*: Silver tinsel and gold twist.
> *Hackle*: A full deep yellow eagle hackle well down body.
> *Shoulder*: Teal.
> *Wing*: Turkey, black and white distinct bars.
> *Head*: Black.

Murdoch followed this up on 30th January 1886 with this quite different pattern, which he attributed to the Oban tackle-maker Mr John Alexander Dunbar:

> *Tag*: Silver thread.
> *Tail*: Sprigs of tippet, or the red rump feather of the golden pheasant.
> *Body*: Scarlet seal's fur, or yellow and scarlet seal's fur in equal joints.
> *Ribbed*: Silver tinsel and silver cord in good bold spirals.
> *Hackle*: From third way down the body, down of the golden eagle dyed a pronounced yellow. The longer and fluffier the fibres are so much the better. Hackle sparse for some rivers, medium for others, but pretty full for most.
> *Wings*: Silver spreckled strips of turkey, with black bar and white tip extending flatwise outward at

an angle of from 15 to 20 degrees from the top of the iron.

Head: Varnished
Dressed on Limericks from 1/0 up to 10/0.

Saturday 22 March: *Fished in evening with ordinary sized water and medium sized flies round by Bridge of Dee without a rise. Put on the large hook described below, and killed two fish with it – one in pool under Wooden Bridge* [a pool on the Balmoral beat of the Dee] *the other being in foot of Garlin. Gold Pheasant crest tip, oval silver tinsel along with broad flat. Body blue spot at tail then yellow, green, blue in equal quantity. Heron grey roll feather, hackle jay. Wings – spotted turkey, with black tips, 3½ inches long,*

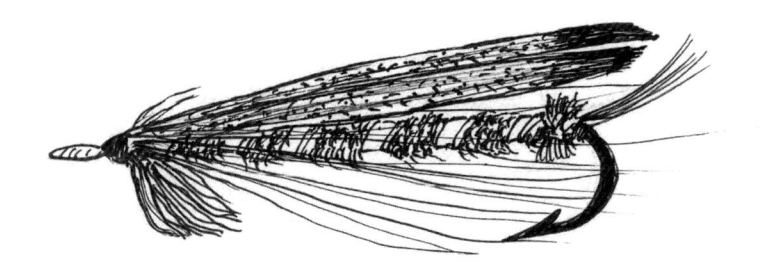

full size hook 3 inches exactly.

The Wooden Brig fly

Of all the flies described by John Michie, the Wooden Brig fly (Figure 3.5) is probably my favourite. It has similarities to other Dee strip wing flies. For example, the blue spot at the tail is similar to the 'Lady of the Lake' (Figure 3.5 and 3.6), one of a set of flies called the Scott Series and brought to the market by Hardy Brothers of Alnwick; however, I have never seen a Dee strip wing with a jay hackle before. In the example illustrated here in Figure 3.5, Eddie has replaced the jay hackle with a blue-dyed guinea fowl feather, as it has proved very difficult to find a feather large enough for this size of hook.

Figure 3.5 On the left the 'Wooden Brig fly' tied by Eddie Kublin on the right a vintage 'Lady of the Lake'

Tail: Golden pheasant crest tippet.
Rib: Oval silver tinsel along with broad flat.
Body: Blue spot at tail then yellow, green, blue in equal quantity.
Hackle: Heron grey roll feather, hackle jay.
Wings: Spotted turkey, with black tips, 3½ inches long.
Hook: Full size, 3 inches exactly. [Roughly equivalent in length to a 9/0 hook]

The Lady of the Lake

The Lady of the Lake (Figures 3.5 and 3.6) is one of a group of flies introduced by Hardy's of Alnwick in the 1920s under the name of the 'Scott Series', each of the six flies being named after one of the Scottish author Sir Walter Scott's popular novels: The Lady of the Lake, Ivanhoe, Waverley, Rob Roy, The Black Dwarf and Marmion.

Hardy's idea was to produce a range of flies that were simpler than standard flies of the day, with low wings, slim bodies and long hackles, a couple of them even using golden pheasant crest feathers as body

Figure 3.6 Lady of the Lake

hackles (harking back to the Gardener and the original Akroyd). Two of the flies in particular were almost reinventions of the Dee strip wing style; these were the Lady of the Lake and the Marmion (which is very similar to the Dunt). The sketch illustration of the Lady of the Lake in Figure 3.6 was taken from a Hardy's catalogue from the 1920s. The pattern details for the Scott Series can be found in the second edition of Hale's *How to Tie Salmon Flies*, published in 1919:

Tag:	Silver flat.
Tail:	Tippet.
Body:	2 turns of blue floss; yellow, orange and black mohair.
Ribs:	Silver flat.
Hackle:	Golden yellow.
Throat:	Golden pheasant breast.
Wings:	Strips of cinnamon turkey.

Saturday 3 May: *Alick Profeit & William Brown* [the brother of Queen Victoria's favourite gillie John Brown] *came in and had some tea. They had been fishing & had got one salmon. I went with them in the evening as far as Garlin but saw no fish. They went down the water while I went up to the old bridge later but all my sport was one rise. Water very clear & moon shining brightly.*

Friday 9 May: *Walked to Dr Profeit's who gave me some prawns & asked me to try for a fish as he had to go to Strathdon to see a horse. Killed a fish in evening not with prawn which I detest to fish with but with very small fly total length of hook being just an inch and composed thus – a few fibres of wild drake for tail; body, hare's ear with fine gold tinsel; hackle grouse; wings jay's wing fibre. This is a favourite small hook*

Good old John, although given prawns to fish with, presumably to guarantee a fish for Dr Profeit's table, he does not use them, but goes out and catches his fish in a much more elegant way (Figure 3.3). This fly fits into the summer or low-water category of fly, almost a March Brown if it were not for the most unusual jay wing.

A Favourite Small Hook

Tail:	A few fibres of wild drake.
Body:	Hare's ear with fine gold tinsel.
Hackle:	Grouse.
Wings:	Jay's wing fibre.
Hook:	1 inch.

Saturday 10 May: *Dr came up afternoon and fished. He caught nothing but I caught one for him with very small eagle & drake wing; body being blue, green & orange & hook 1¼. I fished later & caught largest fish I have got this season it weighing 15 lbs with the hook described on the 22nd of March but smaller being 2¼ inches. Killed another small fish, with hook described yesterday. Water clear but weather dark & mist low.*

Figure 3.7 'A Very Small Eagle fly' tied by Eddie Kublin

A Very Small Eagle fly

Body: Blue, green & orange
Hackle: Eagle.
Wing: Drake.
Hook: 1¼ inches.

This is an example of original thinking applied to fly dressing. It is unusual, but not unheard of, to find small Eagle flies, but I have never seen or heard of an Eagle fly with mallard flank wings before (Figure 3.7).

Salmon flies with green bodies are and have always been very popular in the Scandinavian counties, especially Norway. Green is not a popular colour on the River Dee today; in fact, I have on a couple of occasions, when asking a gillie about the best fly to use, had the response 'ony flee as long as it's nay green.' However, it seemed to be very different in John Michie's time. John used green in quite a few of his flies, and some of the other flies designed for the upper Dee have either been predominately green or have at least had a significant green component. There is the Balmoral with its mostly green body, the similar Monaltrie with its full green body, the Gardener with a green central part to its body, and the Green Charm; the first three (Figure 3.8) follow here and we will get to the Green Charm a little later.

Balmoral

Murdoch published the dressing for the Balmoral (Figure 3.8) three times during the 1880s: first on 23rd February 1884, which was quite reduced: 'Green body, silver tinsel, black hackle, jungle cock, red wings, and golden pheasant tail,' and then on 23rd February of the same year, as shown here:

Tag: Silver tinsel and orange floss.
Tail: A topping and fibres of golden pheasant tippet.
Body: Three turns green, and two turns black mohair.
Ribbed: Silver tinsel and gold twist.
Hackle: Black heron well down body.
Cheeks: Jungle cock feather on either cheek.
Wing: Dark brown turkey with black tips.
Head: Black.

Finally, on 3rd April 1886, Murdoch gave the following variations and instructions:

Tag: Silver twist. [misses out the orange floss]
Tail: A topping and pintail. [substitutes pintail for fibres of golden pheasant tippet]
Butt: Black ostrich. [this is new]
Body: Bright green and black mohair – two thirds of the former to one third of the latter.
Ribbed: Silver tinsel [flat] and silver cord. [changes the colour of the cord from gold to silver]

Hackle: Black heron of the longest fibre – from bright green mohair. [a more specific starting point for the hackle]
Shoulder: Teal – sparingly. [this is new]
Wings: Strips of cream coloured turkey feather extending flatwise outward from the top of the iron at an angle of 15 degrees. [changes the colour of the turkey and give more precise instructions of how the wings should lie]
Cheeks: Jungle.
Head: Varnished.

Monaltrie

The pattern for this Dee strip wing fly was given to me by Colin Simpson, a gillie on the Lower Blackhall beat of the River Dee and collector of salmon fly patterns (Figure 3.8).

Monaltrie (translating as 'moor of the hillside') is a beat on the upper part of the River Dee just below the Queen's Birkhall beat. It is also the name of a large country house where James Harper (senior) was working as a gardener when he invented the Gardener fly. The Monaltrie fly is of interest due to the colour of the body and the treatment of the tail, which is almost shrimp fly-like:

Tag: Oval silver.
Tail: Golden pheasant red breast wound.
Body: Grass green mohair or seal, rib broad flat tinsel.
Hackle: Black heron.
Throat: Teal.
Wing: Barred turkey.

Figure 3.8 "Green Flies" from the top clockwise: vintage Balmoral, vintage Gardener, Monaltrie tied by Eddie Kublin and another vintage Gardener

72

Gardener

In most books about the salmon fly, the Gardener (Figure 3.8) has been attributed to William Garden, fishing tackle-maker of Aberdeen. This inaccuracy was probably initiated by Kelson in his book *The Salmon Fly*, published in 1895, where he states that the dressing of the Gardener came from William Garden. I have never been sure whether this was intentional, as Kelson does not explicitly say that Garden was the inventor, instead describing 'one of Garden's best Dee flies.' The name 'Gardener' also would give weight to this view. However, as the *Fishing Gazette* highlighted no fewer than three times (twice before Kelson published *The Salmon Fly*) that the Gardener was invented by James Harper. It is amazing that modern researchers still stick to Kelson's initial confusion.

The *Fishing Gazette*'s first mention of this fly was when Mr Marston published an obituary for Francis Harper in 1889 (Francis being James's brother and a well-respected fisherman of the Dee). This included the statement 'His favourite flies were the Heron (with red wing), the Gardener (invented by his brother James), Jock Scott, Popham, Eagle (with mottled turkey wing), Gordon, Akroyd, Silver Doctor, Black Doctor, and Thunderer, and almost invariably the White Eagle was the fly with which he closed the day.'

The second mention was in an article in the series 'Famous Fishermen' by 'MAC', on 29th March 1890. James Harper was the subject, and the article started with the introduction:

> Amongst the masters of the gentle art on Dee-side, which well can boast of at least half a score of as competent professional salmon anglers as anywhere to be found, Mr James Harper, of the church-square, Ballater, familiarly known as "the Gardener," takes a foremost place. Harper is indeed a keen, a fine and a fortunate fisher.

The article continues with a description of James and his progression through life, starting as an apprentice gardener at Borrowstone House, Kincardine O'Neil:

> He often had the run of the water to himself for almost the whole

of the season, and one year his agreement was that he would fish the water and do the garden work for half of the fish he might kill.' James eventually took up the position of gardener at Monaltrie House in Ballater, employed by Mr Fred Pickop, and in 1882 started up his own tackle-making business in Ballater, with a branch in Braemar. Over time, the business grew and became James Harper & Son, Fishmongers & Gamedealers, Fruiterers, Florists & Greengrocers, with shops in Ballater and Braemar.

James Harper's favourite flies included 'the Grey Eagle, Yellow Eagle, Gordon, Dunt, Gardener, White Wing, Jock Scott, Childers, Yellow Gaudie, Grey Heron, Akroyd, Silver Doctor, Black Doctor, Green Peacock, Blue Charm, Jeannie, and Logie.' The really interesting part of this article is the following quote from Harper: 'I may also state that I am the inventor of the Gardener, the Craigendarroch Butterfly, and a white fly – a very good evening fly – which Mr. Fred Pickop, my late master, christened the Monaltrie Owl.' Although we know the pattern for the Gardener, those for the Craigendarroch Butterfly and the Monaltrie Owl are currently lost. There is a Dee strip wing fly called the Monaltrie, but it is predominantly green in colour rather than white.

In 1907, there was a very public spat between Marston of the *Fishing Gazette* and Kelson of *The Salmon Fly*, one of the bones of contention being that Kelson had incorrectly credited himself with the invention of a quantity of salmon flies, and that he had also incorrectly attributed flies to some of his cronies. James Harper's nephew, the son of Francis Harper and also called James (who was the proprietor of William Brown's tackle business in Aberdeen from 1901), entered into correspondence with Marston. In one of his letters, James let his feelings be known:

> I have not the personal acquaintance of G.M.K. [Kelson] and would shy of it, but am familiar with his identity from my old Bernard [a well respected London tackle house where James Junior learned his trade] days in the early eighties. He has not left kindly impressions here nor on Spey. I marvel at the anxiety of some Angling writers for the credit of

invention. Pennell [author of several books on fishing] seems another case. The obvious shallowness of much of the quibbling must undermine any real claim they could establish for respect from future generations. G.M.K.s "Salmon Fly" and his long list of fearfully overdressed "inventions" is not to my liking. I recall to mind one error by him. He ascribes the "Gardener" to Garden. This fly was "invented" – to repeat his, in such case, ridiculous term – by my uncle James Harper while Gardener at Monaltrie [House], Ballater. There was, I believe, a real novelty here in the use of the Golden Pheasant Topping as a hackle. Well do I remember my boyish difficulty to get this to lie smoothly.

This correspondence led to Marston publishing 'Salmon Fly Histories – The Inventor of the "Gardener" Salmon Fly' in the *Fishing Gazette* on 7th March 1908:

The invention of that handsome and killing Dee salmon fly, the 'Gardener,' is ascribed by Mr. Kelson to Mr. Garden. The real inventor was Mr. James Harper, when he was gardener at Monaltrie House, Ballater, thirty-six years ago. Mr. Harper made three, and gave one to his brother, Mr. John Harper, of Dess, one to Wilkinson, who was then fishing at Monaltrie, and kept one himself. Four fish were killed with them in one day, and the gentleman who was fishing with John Harper sent to the gardener for eighteen more, same as the first pattern. James Harper was out of feathers, and he sent the order to Mr. Blacklaws, of Kincardine O'Neil, who will doubtless remember the incident. The 'Gardener' has since been a favourite Dee pattern; and is a very taking one from the Angler's point of view. It is well dressed, to please the inventor, by his nephew, Mr. James Harper (Junior), the present proprietor of the well-known old business of Wm. Brown and Co., of George-street, Aberdeen, inventors of the celebrated Phantom Minnow. Mr James Harper is a salmon angler himself, and his flies are deservedly favourites.

From this article, it can be established that the Gardener was 'invented' in 1872 and predates the Akroyd (which also utilised golden pheasant tippet as a hackle) by three years.

The pattern given below is as described by Murdoch in the *Fishing Gazette* on 16th February 1884:

Tag: Silver tinsel and orange floss.
Tail: A topping and fibres of golden pheasant tippet.
Body: Two turns orange, two turns green, and four turns purple mohair.
Rib: Silver tinsel and gold twist.
Hackle: Large topping down the body.
Shoulder: Black heron hackle.
Cheeks: Jungle cock.
Wings: Dark brown turkey.
Head: Black.

Friday 16 May: *Caught a salmon with very small fly – drake tail, thread silver tinsel, orange body (pig's wool) partridge hackle, woodcock wings.*

A Very Small Fly

This is the only pattern where John Michie gives the material of the body as well as the colour of the body. This suggests that the other flies would have been made either from mohair or seal's fur, and of these mohair was probably the more commonly used material in the late 1800s on Deeside. This is a fairly typical summer or low-water fly (almost a trout fly! See Figure 3.9):

Tail: Drake.
Rib: Silver tinsel.
Body: Orange (pig's wool).
Hackle: Partridge.
Wing: Woodcock.

Figure 3.9 A Very Small Fly tied by Eddie Kublin and some vintage Clunies

1891

Wednesday 27 May: *At the Castle in forepart of day. In the afternoon got home. Prince Henry of Battenberg* [husband of Princess Beatrice, Queen Victoria's youngest daughter] *having gone to fish after lunch and having broken his rod sent for mine. I went to the Garlin pool with it where HRH caught a fish of 13 lbs the only rise got. The Grand Duke was also out with Donald Stewart* [a retired head gamekeeper still living on the estate] *but he was clean.*

Monday 1 June: *The Officer of the Scots Guards* [a regiment that forms the Guard of Honour to the Queen], *who was accidentally drowned near Pool Vere* [now more commonly known as Polvier, a pool on the Birkhall beat of the Dee; its name means 'the Bailie's pool'], *on the Birkhall water while fishing the other day was removed from Ballater today. The Queen, Princes & part of household went to the funeral as did most of the inhabitants of Ballater.*

Tuesday 7 July: *Started for the Glassalt Shiel* ['a cottage residence' on the banks of Loch Muick built in 1868 by Queen Victoria shortly after becoming a widow] *having first visited the fencers on Cairn Taggart, fished Loch Buie and got thoroughly wet to the skin from several thunder showers. In the loch caught about 3 dozen of well shaped trout weighing about 6 to the pound. On arrival at Glassalt found Campbell was from home and could get no change of clothing in consequence. At last however a pair of his trousers was found in a parcel as well as stockings and I managed with the assistance of a good fire. Had a comfortable bed & slept well.*

Wednesday 8 July: *Got up about 8 am and found a pouring morning of rain which improved between 9 & 10 o'clock. I started rod in hand for Altnagiubhsaich* [usually written Allt-na-Giubhsaich, built by Queen Victoria as a 'get away'] *to find that Cameron had gone a fishing to the Muick. He returned however while I looked round the place but would not accompany me as I expected he would to the Loch of Lochnagar. I started for it alone and arrived on its banks at 1.30. Caught 21 trout 3 of which I rejected on account of being badly shaped. The remaining 18 weighed 8½ lbs. There were two distinct species one being of a yellowish brown colour, generally of a fairly good shape, while the other was of a silvery hue outside, pink flesh and beautiful mould. They seemed to take in about equal numbers.*

1892

Thursday 11 February: *The snow however is now entirely away and the weather dry, fine and windy. Had a cast at the fishing, this day being the opening, but got no rises. It is not known whether clean salmon have got up this distance from the sea this year yet. McIntosh by the way said he had a rise in McLaren's pool* [a pool on the Balmoral beat of the River Dee] *on his way up.*

Friday 4 March: *Fished in the afternoon and landed a kelt in the afternoon in the Red Brae* [a pool on the Abergeldie beat of the

Dee] *when every fish in the pool could be seen from the bank head. David* [John Michie's eldest son who was eleven years old at the time.] *saw this one rise from the bottom take the fly and return. It was as usual when he turned to go that I felt the line tight. There were several more fish lying at the same place but we failed to distinguish whether clean or foul. Weather continues frosty. Wind easterly.*

Monday 14 March: *Ludwig IV Grand Duke of Hesse who was married to Princess Alice 2nd daughter of the Queen died at 1.15 am yesterday (Sunday). The Grand Duke was a very frequent visitor at Balmoral the last occasion being during the Queen's stay in May & June of last year when I had the honour of shooting with him several times. He was much liked by all here with whom he came in contact. When here last summer he fished in the Dee several times and wore the kilt which dress became him well from his stout manly proportionate build. The news reached us this (Monday) morning.*

Saturday 19 March: *Fished in the evening and killed my first salmon on the season having landed a kelt only before. Weather frosty again several degrees being registered.*

Wednesday 15 June: *Prince George of Wales* [Duke of York just created] *is fishing here today. Weather still very cold.*

Monday 11 July: *Saw Garden, Gunmaker of Aberdeen* [William Garden of Aberdeen was also a fishing tackle-maker and is quoted by Kelson in *The Salmon Fly*] *there who had come to see Cameron taking advantage of the shopkeepers' holiday. Found Campbell and took sizes of wood for construction of new fishing piers*

Saturday 20 August: *Attended by invitation Dr Profeit's net fishing at Loch Muick which is annual matter. Sir A McKenzie & Lady were about till lunch when they went home. Dr Ogston and Mr Garden of Chalmers, 13 Union Terrace were there and the gamekeepers.*

Net fishing on Loch Muick was a social occasion and would often involve a picnic. One end of a long net would be attached to a rowing boat, which would then be rowed out into the loch in a large circle, dragging the net behind it. Once the boat reached shore again, the royal guests and staff would wade into the water and pull the net in, making the circle smaller and smaller until the fish could be scooped out. Trout deemed worthy of the table would be kept, and smaller fish would be put back.

Friday 30 September: The Princess of Wales has taken to salmon fishing lately and caught several fish on the Invercauld water [the beat on the opposite side of the river to Abergeldie, which translates as 'infall of the small burn'] *these days.*

Saturday 5 November: After going my rounds among my men met Mr Pirie Overseer at Blackhall Castle [an estate near Banchory on the banks of the River Dee; the castle was demolished in 1947 and the fishing lodge for the Little Blackhall beat now sits on the site] *showed him over the Policy grounds. Mr Francis Clark took him round by the cottages and distillery* [Royal Lochnagar, situated close to Balmoral Castle] *in the darkening while I got a dogcart from the stables and proceed home to don evening kilt dress to be present at a repetition of the Thursday evening's proceedings at which the Queen was again present. Drove Mr Pirie to the Danzig in the evening late where he spends the night with me. Weather fine. Pirie is an enthusiastic forester and possessed a good deal of knowledge concerning the management of woods. He is also somewhat of a gardener as well as a farmer and boasts to some little extent of his quality as a plain gun shot. This list if you add a good salmon angler, means that Mr Pirie knows a good deal about the management of a country place of the higher-flying type.*

In 1845, John Begg was granted a long lease of the Lochnagar site by the Abergeldie Estate to build a distillery; in 1848, Prince Albert visited it and was so impressed that he asked Queen Victoria to visit it the next day. They watched the process and sampled the end product, enjoying it so much that the Queen bestowed the title of 'Royal Lochnagar.' Today the distillery is under the ownership of Diageo Scotland Limited, which employs six members of staff to run the traditional distilling process.

1893

Saturday 11 February: The salmon fishing opened today. The day was open weather with a full river fished McLaren's pool but landed 1 kelt only. C McIntosh [Underkeeper on the estate] *had another. Hear, however the keepers below killed between Abergeldie & Ballater 3 clean fish. Under the average takes all the way down the river are reported, and the nets about the mouth are no better.*

Saturday 18 February: Fished Garlin in the evening but without success. When at Dr Profeit's at 12.30 pm his son George came in with 2 fine clean fish from Clachanturn [a pool on the Abergeldie beat of the River Dee, which translates as 'stone of the hill'] *whither he had gone in course of the morning.*

Tuesday 25 April: Went to Birkhall. Directed James Duguid to erect fence at Knocks mill dam. Beat carpets at hut and then commence to tidy up roads in preparation for the Queen's coming. On arrival home had the best fishing experienced this season – went out 7.10 pm and returned indoors at 9.30 with 4 salmon and a trout. Salmon averaged 7½ lbs. Weather quiet and cloudy, mild. Moon which however was not shining. Hooks – Jock Scot killed 2 before darkness after which a black heron with orange & black body and red wing of large size later.

This diary entry has caused me quite a lot of confusion; on first reading it, I interpreted 'a black heron with orange & black body and red wing of large size' as 'a Black Heron with an orange and back body and with large red wings.' After thought and discussion, it

Figure 3.10 The Red Wing (*left*) and Rintoul, both tied by Eddie Kublin

seems to make more sense that this should be interpreted as 'A Black Heron (with an orange and black body) and (later) a large Red Wing' – the Red Wing is a recognised Dee strip wing pattern.

John Michie's 'Black Heron' also fits into the category of the Dee strip wing and, looking at the patterns of the known Dee strip wings, there is a very close match in the black heron hackled fly, the 'Rintoul'.

Rintoul

The dressing for the Rintoul (Figure 3.10) first appeared in one of William Murdoch's pieces on the Dee, published in the *Fishing Gazette* on 16th February 1884. The following addition was given by Murdoch on 8th March 1884, also in the *Fishing Gazette*: 'The dressing of the "Rintoul," previously described, may, if desired, be supplemented by a little golden pheasant rump around the shoulder. We, however, prefer this fly, minus the addition indicated.' The following from the Scottish Field of March 1908 gives some indication of where the Rintoul may have originated:

Old Rintoul at Crathes was another famous all-round man. He sallied out with the rod over his shoulder, and was easily recognised at a distance by his bell-topper hat. He was a worthy man, a keeper of the "old gentleman" school. He always carried a big "doss" of fine seals' which dangled from the leather tab to which his watch was attached. He could catch fish with any man, especially if fish were a bit stiff to put up. He has told the writer how, when repeatedly baffled, he would sit down on the big stone at the top of Buhoar pool and tie a fly that the salmon could not resist. He was mightily fond of the Peacock Heron fly. Quite a number of the most noted killing Dee flies of those days were invented by Rintoul and George Robbie.

Tag: Silver tinsel.
Tail: A topping and fibres of golden pheasant tippet.
Body: Two turns orange and three turns black mohair.
Rib: Silver tinsel and gold twist.
Hackle: Black heron down the body.
Cheeks: Jungle cock.
Wing: Sand coloured turkey.
Head: Black.

Red Wing

The dressing for the Red Wing (Figure 3.10) given below is the accepted pattern first published in the *Fishing Gazette* on 16th February 1884, subsequently appearing on 14th March the following year and again on 3rd March 1888. The dressing remained constant, but the 1888 pattern gives more information on the shape of the wing: 'Two strips of the darkest brown turkey feather procurable, each extending flatwise outward at an angle of 25–30 degrees.'

Murdoch goes on to give a little on the history of the fly:

The Red Wing fly is one of a few patterns used on Dee, Don, Deveron, Ythan, and several other northern rivers, that while possessing old and familiar names telling of well-authenticated stunning records of genuine sport, had gradually fallen into disuse as the years rolled on and new "blood" came on the scene, until only a few years ago they had almost wholly died out among the then anglers, when, as if all of a sudden, by several of the most successful and intelligent rods, desirous to try the cherished patterns of their fathers in the art, they were revived, and with some alterations (which are considered improvements) were brought out under the old names, and their bringing, as it has done, such immense success to those using them has made their re-introduction as popular, as popular and good friends all were the worthy old hands who first used them. The Red Wing is the invention of dear "Old Dusty," now, alas, no more; a keen and true angler in every sense, eager ever for sport himself and as eagerly bent and solicitous for others having it, and than whom no more genial companion, friend, and guide, versed in flies, fishing, fish lore, and fishes' ways, one could have had or wished at the river side. These lines are penned not without feeling, and are a brief and feeble but well-merited tribute to the memory of one of a class of fishermen that is fast passing away.

The Red Wing is not a summer fly, but either in spring or autumn it does admirably, used in from low to fairly high water, the size of course [of the fly] being suitable, and chiefly on darkish days is it most telling. Mr. Jopp, the well known angler, pays it a high tribute in saying that on the Deveron "it takes fish both inside and outside the mouth!" and that for that river "he places it in front of any other fly." On many occasions the writer has had great sport with it on the Aberdeenshire Dee, and it is the companion fly of the "Dr. Forbes," invented by Dr. Forbes, of Liverpool, a gentleman who has fished with most distinguished success on Dee, Don, Brora, Shin and many other rivers, north and south. The dressing given to us by Mr. William Garden, tackle maker, 122½ Union Street, Aberdeen.

Tag: Silver tinsel.
Tail: Fibres of golden pheasant tippet.
Body: Blue and claret mohair.

Rib: Silver tinsel. [14th March 1884: broad flat silver tinsel and silver twist, five turns; 3rd March 1888: broad flat silver tinsel, edged with gold twist (treble)]
Hackle: Grey heron well through the body.
Shoulder: Teal.
Wing: Very dark turkey, the deeper the brown the better.
Head: Black.

Doctor Forbes

The following pattern comes from John James Hardy's *Salmon Fishing* (1907).

Tag: Flat gold tinsel.
Tail: Golden pheasant crest and tippets.
Butt: Black ostrich.
Body: Rear half, bright orange silk, front, black silk.
Rib: Gold and silver tinsel.
Hackle: Black heron over black silk.
Throat: Golden pheasant red body hackle.
Wing: Dark mottled turkey.

1894

Tuesday 30 January: *At sawmills and in afternoon dressing salmon flies.*

Monday 12 February: *Arthur Grant* [Second Keeper] *was at the Smithy ready to fish whenever the river cleared of grue* ['grue' is the Scots word for floating ice in the river] *which it did afternoon but he got no salmon nor anybody else above McKenzie's water of Glen Muick there a heavy fish was landed.*

Tuesday 27 February: Donald Stewart killed a small salmon in Pool Moniere [now better known as Polmonier is a pool on the Balmoral beat; it translates as 'Saint Manear's pool'] *yesterday, the first one so far up the river this season. It was 6 lbs. Arthur Grant has got 2 at Clachanturn and below but they are heavy fish being 21 and 19 lbs respectively – a bad sign it is reckoned for quality.*

Friday 2 March: Boisterous weather from the westward prevails with double sway but toward evening the wind moderated. In the after noon had a cast for a fish which after unsuccessful attempts at the Auld Brig [a pool on the Balmoral beat of the Dee], *Red Brae, & Wooden Brig I got in Garlin about 4 pm with a plain grey heron with spotted turkey wings – the first fish of the season weighing 16 lbs at a time too when I was inclined to the popular opinion that there were none in the river so far up. Very large quantities of snow on the hills although a considerable quantity lay on the ground this forenoon by mid-day it had mostly disappeared.*

The Grey Heron

The Grey Heron (Figure 3.11) is a standard Dee strip wing fly first listed as a relatively 'plain' pattern by Murdoch in the *Fishing Gazette* on 16th February 1884:

> *Tag*: Gold tinsel.
> *Tail*: A topping and golden pheasant tippet (small).
> *Body*: Orange mohair, well picked out.
> *Rib*: Gold tinsel.
> *Hackle*: Grey heron.
> *Shoulder*: Teal.
> *Wing*: Mottled turkey, brownish tinge.
> *Head*: Black.

Murdoch went on to list a more complex dressing in *Fishing Gazette* on 14th March 1885:

Figure 3.11 The Grey Heron tied by Eddie Kublin

Tag: Gold thread and topping-coloured floss silk.
Tail: Fibres of tippet.
Body: Orange-coloured pig's wool or mohair (the former by preference), well picked out.
Ribbed: Broad flat gold tinsel and gold twist, five turns.
Hackle: Long grey heron, wound openly round body.
Shoulder: Teal.
Wings: Either cream-coloured turkey strips, or distinctly barred black and white turkey strips.
Head: Black.

Murdoch's commentary on the fly continued with:
Mr. George Smith, Tackle Merchant, Ballater, has a splendid stock of these patterns, most of which are proved killers on all reaches above, and a good many reaches below, that place.
As Michie stated that it was a 'plain' Grey Heron that he used, I think it was probably the first of Murdoch's patterns.

Friday 27 April: Fished in the evening without the least sign of a rise. Had a cast however by chance in the middle of the day in the Red Brae pool with small clear water & sunshine with a small Jock Scott with which caught a fish.

Jock Scott

There cannot be many rivers in the world that hold salmon that have not had a Jock Scott (Figure 2.2) cast into them. The Jock Scott is easily the most famous classic salmon fly, and John Michie mentions using it successfully on the River Dee in his diary. There are many different accounts of the invention of the Jock Scott, but they all attribute the fly to Jock Scott, who was the fisherman to Lord John Scott. I particularly like the version of the fly's creation published in the *Scotsman* newspaper on the 17th September 1926 by the Reverend William McCallum:

> The date of its birth in 1850. In that year Lord John Scott rented Makerstoun water from Sir Thomas Macdougall Brisbane, laird of Makerstoun at the time. Tho' autumn was disappointing, there were fish, but anglers could not catch them. The fisherman set himself to devise something new; the result was the Jock Scott, which Kelson has pronounced "the acknowledged king of built-wing flies, fit to reign over his own large circle of admirers." No one taught the inventor the art he enriched. When a boy just into his teens he began work at Monteviot and with a spare half-crown he bought an Irish fly, which he carefully stripped, and dressed again. Afterwards a gentleman on his return from the East gave him feathers of the Indian crow, jungle cock, and macaw, which are among the twenty-seven items that make up the fly. Though like nothing in Nature, the markings of the Red Admiral butterfly suggested to his mind the use of jungle cock for the sides of the fly, while for the head he took the hair of his beard, which was black, as he was then but three and thirty years of age. After trying it on the sporting pools of Makerstoun, he gave a pattern to the Duke of Roxburghe and to Mr. Forrest, Kelso, who, being successful with

it, christened it "Jock Scott." Perhaps it was the fact of the busker's [fly-dresser's] beard being in the fly that led Mr. Forrest to give it his name. At any rate, when the Duchess of Roxburghe heard that it was with a fly dressed with the hair of the Makerstoun fisherman's beard that His Grace was catching salmon, she drove up to see the inventor and inquire of him as to the truth of the story.

The following is the earliest (and simplest, so would appeal to a practical fly-tier like John Michie) published pattern for the Jock Scott; it appeared in *A Book on Angling* by Francis Francis in 1867 when the pattern was still relatively new. Francis describes it as 'Another good Tweed pattern, which is very useful elsewhere':

Tag: Gold twist.
Tail: One topping and one Indian crow feather.
Body: In two joints, gold coloured floss the lowest, and black ross the upper; from the joint is tied, after the fashion of the Popham, two or three short toucan points, and over the buts of them, at the joint, two turns of black herl; silver twist, a black hackle over the black joint.
Shoulder: Speckled Gallina.
Wings: Mixed, a white tip turkey slip in the middle, fibres of pintail, or teal, bustard, brown mallard, yellow, red and green parrot, one topping over all.
Cheeks: Kingfisher.
Horns: Blue macaw.

FISHERMAN'S MAP
OF SALMON POOLS
on the River DEE by
MAUDE PARKER, R.W.A.
Scale—1 Inch to 1 Mile.
1931.

Akroyd

The Akroyd (Figure 3.12, A1 and A.5) is one of if not the most famous of the Dee strip wings. It is often described as the 'poor man's Jock Scott' as it gives the impression of the yellow and black body of the Jock Scott.

The fly was invented by Charles Akroyd in 1875. As Murdoch did not include Akroyd's ribbing in the pattern he published in 1884, I have included the details recorded by Pryce-Tannatt in his important 1914 work *How to Dress Salmon Flies*. The dressing stated was probably how the fly was being tied in 1884, but the original fly was tied with golden pheasant topping in place of the yellow hackle, as Akroyd states in *A Veteran Sportsman's Diary*, published in 1926: 'It is not dressed now in quite the same way as when I dressed it. Where the fly-dressers now use a cock's hackle dyed yellow, I put in two long golden pheasant's crest feathers running all the way down, my idea being that the glitter was more attractive than the dull hackle.'

Tag: Gold tinsel.
Tail: A topping and golden pheasant tippet.
Body: Yellow and black mohair in equal proportion.
Ribs: Oval silver tinsel over the orange seal's fur; flat silver tinsel and twist over black floss.
Hackle: Yellow hackle over yellow mohair and black heron hackle over black mohair.
Cheeks: Jungle cock.
Wing: White or brown turkey.
Head: Black.

Kelson describes in *The Salmon Fly* (1895): 'An excellent Dee pattern. For early fishing in snow water this fly is often dressed with double white wings; the first pair (strips) at centre of body, the others at head. This variation has proved of much service on many rivers, and was introduced some years ago by Garden, of Aberdeen.' (Figure 3.13)

(Opposite) Figure 3.12 A collection of vintage Akroyds

Figure 3.13 A vintage Double White Winged Akroyd

1896

Tuesday 11 February: *This day being opening of the fishing on the Dee had a cast & killed.*

Thursday 13 February: *Saw a Colonel Blackett who has taken Invercauld home fishing who had landed 6 clean salmon today.*

Tuesday 25 February: *Weather fair with a frost & wind from south. Killed a salmon at 5.30 pm in small clear water with small sized Jock Scott while ice was crisping on the line.*

Friday 28 February: A boisterously windy day, keen and cold. Fished from 4 to 5 pm without any hope of a rise on account of the strong gusty, bitterly cold wind. To my surprise landed 2 salmon every circumstance being unpropitious [sic]. Water very small & clear.

1897

Saturday 27 February: Received a message from Donald Stewart through Charles McIntosh not to fish meantime except on Saturdays, which I do not mean to comply with & also that two salmon boxes had been seen leaving by Post Car from me, which is without foundation. D Stewart's message had it that these boxes were seen by Mr Leopold Profeit [graduate of the University of Aberdeen, aspiring actor and son of Alexander Profeit; he held the rank of Captain and died in 1917 in Lake Doiran, Greece] and Reid the Balmoral policeman.

Tuesday 2 March: Saw Donald Stewart at the Boat Pool [a pool on the Birkhall beat of the River Dee] after having called at his house and informed him that I would fish as before, and threatened to raise an action against him for defamation of character.

Friday 19 March: Drove to Invergelder [a small farmhouse on the banks of the Gelder, a tributary of the River Dee; Gelder translates as 'clear water burn' – it is interesting to note that there is a footbridge over the Gelder called Michie's bridge], where workmen are engaged preparing Castle firewood. Met Leopold Profeit there who had a call from Donald Stewart in answer to a letter charging Stewart for defaming him. The result of Stewart having sent a message to me by McIntosh that Leopold had seen two fish boxes in transit from me by Post Car, which was not the case, and is just a trumped up lie. I went with Leopold at his wish to Stewart's but nothing was arrived at now we have demanded McIntosh's presence at 10 am tomorrow.

Saturday 20 March: *Went to Invergelder where put in my horse and met Mr Leopold Profeit at Donald Stewart's, McIntosh having been there before. Had some unpleasant argument in which Stewart and McIntosh denied their words. Instead of clearing up the matter it became more complicated and I left in disgust Leopold following convinced that they would perjure themselves anywhere as they had done then.*

Monday 19 April: *Got my first fish of the season, a small one, very late.*

Thursday 23 September: *To Balmoral to meet Mr Forbes who was to have driven me to Birkhall but couldn't get away on account of being busy at the Castle. Had lunch with the Forbes and drove home afternoon to find BJO but he did not arrive till after father, David of Ceylon* [John Michie's brother] *& I had gone down to Garlin to try a cast at the senior's request. He went over the stream from north side when about half a dozen fish rose at his fly, two of which he hooked but lost. I then tried it over with the same fly & rose one almost at once which did not hook. In a few seconds after a queer incident occurred. A big fish rose on his own account just as my line had alighted on the water indeed he jumped on the line about 6 feet nearer than the hook when I at once pulled & hooked him in the body but first through one of the under fins situated a few inches in front of the tail and after a difficult and rather dull run downstream landed what turned out to be a 19 pounder.*

1901

On Tuesday 22nd January Queen Victoria died at Osborne House on the Isle of Wight. On the 28th January, John Michie, as Leader of the Balmoral Highlanders and three of the other Balmoral Highlanders, travelled on the overnight train to London. They then crossed the Solent to the Isle of Wight.

On 1st February, after many rehearsals, they marched with the funeral procession from Osborne House to the Solent from where they crossed to the mainland by boat. The Balmoral Highlanders then travelled by train to Windsor. Meanwhile the Queen's coffin was taken by train to London then to Windsor the following morning.

On 2nd February, the funeral procession marched from Windsor Railway Station to St George's Chapel, Windsor Castle where the Queen's Funeral Service was held.

John Michie's diaries record, in great detail, his experiences and observations made during five momentous and significant days.

> *Wednesday 6th March:* Received a letter from Lt. Co. Sir F.I. Edwards K.C.B. forwarding me a Faithful Service medal and informing me that it was one of the last commands given by Queen Victoria that I be provided with it – still another proof of the thoughtful kindness of our beloved Queen which I appreciate and value more than it is possible to say.

> *Friday 12 April:* Fished in the evening landing my first salmon of the season. Weather – the sun shone brightly afternoon putting away part of the snow of last night & this morning and frost set in recently towards dusk causing my line to freeze in the rod rings; rose three separate fish notwithstanding.

> *Saturday 17 August:* Was officially informed by Sir D.M. Probyn G.C.V.O. etc. etc. Keeper of H.M. Privy Purse, that the King has been graciously pleased to appoint me successor to James Forbes Esquire M.V.O. Commissioner, at Balmoral. My title will be Factor instead of Commissioner.

> *Friday 30 August: To Crathie* [a small village on the north bank of the River Dee, its name meaning 'wooded place'] *in the morning having cycled down got back at noon and met at the Danzig Mr. Harvey brother of Canon Harvey prepared for fishing. We fished Garlin and killed 3 fish. Mr. H 2 & I one.*

> *Thursday 17 October:* At Balmoral waiting the King's commands but His Majesty decided to see me at 5-30 pm along with Sir D.

Probyn and Mr. Forbes. *In the forenoon the King told Mr Forbes that he decided to give me the house of Abergeldie Mains as a residence instead of Craig-Gowans as first arranged.*

Monday 21 October: *By command of the King went to the Castle at 11 am and along with Sir D. Probyn, Major Fredericks, Mr Forbes, Mr James Armstrong and Mr James Reid went through certain portions of the castle with the King who decided on a number of alterations. H.M. afterwards went round the grounds with me. The King presented me with the Victoria Medal for services to the late Queen as Forester. Their Majesties left Balmoral for the south.*

1902

Thursday 20 March: *Weather somewhat rough, but Lord Romney killed a salmon.*

Wednesday 26 March: *The Earl of Romney, and General Home left Craig-Gowan for the Hirsel, Coldstream. N.B. They have caught only one salmon each in course of their weeks fishing. The weather has been of the worst for fishing.*

1903

Wednesday 11 February: *Fished being the opening day but saw nothing. All the keepers at it but Abercromby only got a fish of about 10 lbs in Polhollick* [a pool on the Abergeldie beat of the River Dee, which translates as 'pool of the old woman']. *Water in flood.*

Wednesday 11 March: *Caught my first salmon of the season.*

Friday 6 November: *Attended Meeting of Dee Salmon Fishing Improvement Association, Lord Huntly* [of Aboyne Castle] *presiding. I was proposed by him to go on the Acting Committee* [sic].

Figure 3.14 Bhaile-na-Choile, John Michie's final house on the Balmoral estate. Although the house was originally built for the Queen's favourite servant, John Brown, he never lived there

1904

The Michie family moved from Abergeldie Mains to Bhaile-na-Choile (Figure 3.14.). The current Factor and his family live here today.

> *Wednesday 29th June:* Went to Birkhall in the afternoon where I met Stewart & the other man John Brown handed me the key of Bhaile - na - choile (sic).

1905

> *Tuesday 2nd May:* Drive to Ballater in the morning and met Prince Arthur of Connaught [the Queen's youngest surviving son] who comes to fish accompanied by his Equerry Captain Wyndham. They stay with us at the mains for about 12 days.

> *Thursday 4 May:* Prince Arthur of Connaught and Captain Wyndham went to Cambus o'May [a beat further down river,

between Ballater and Aboyne] *to fish H.R.H. landed one salmon, Captain Wyndham, nothing.*

Friday 5 May: *Walked out in the evening to see Prince Arthur & Captain Wyndham fish. The Prince had a 'rise' while the Captain had a fish on but lost him. I rose one but he did not touch. Weather fine.*

Monday 8 May: *Prince Arthur left for Dinnet [a small village five miles west of Aboyne and the name of the beat there] also Captain Wyndham to fish with Mr. Percy Laming* [in 1897 one of the first to experiment with 'greased line' fishing, prior to A H E Wood in 1903] *with the intention of staying overnight at Profeit's Hotel* [a hotel in Dinnet run by Dr Alexander Profeit's two daughters and now called the Loch Kinord Hotel] *and returning tomorrow night. Wind North, scorching and cold.*

Tuesday 9 May: *Weather fine. The Prince & Equerry returned by afternoon train. They got no salmon at Dinnet.*

Wednesday 10 May: *Weather dull. Prince Arthur got one fish & Captain Wyndham two – the first he ever landed.*

Thursday 11 May: *Attended to correspondence after and then saw Prince Arthur of Connaught and his Equerry Captain Wyndham off for London. During their stay with us the Prince got 6 fish and the Captain 2 fish. They came on the 2nd and expressed the wish they could have stayed a week longer.*

Beatrice, the Michie's 22-year-old youngest daughter had been unwell for some time. She was admitted to The Northern Nursing Home 5 Albyn Place in Aberdeen on 8th June.

"**Thursday 8th June:** *Started with Mrs and Beatrice [in a] Coutts Landau* [Coutts were the local carriage "taxi" firm and a Landau is a type of four-wheeled, convertible, horse drawn carriage] *to* *catch 12.5 train at Ballater. At Aberdeen we brought carriage on to platform and dragged out to roadway and then on to 5 Albyn Place.*

Monday 12th June: *Saw Dr Ogston who I am thankful to say is now sanguine of success in operating on Beatrice's neck which he intends to do on Wednesday. I pray that he is right.*

Beatrice died on Wednesday June 14th. This was the last entry in the 1905 Diary. The Diaries resumed on 1st January 1906.

1906

Tuesday 23 January: *Left for Aberdeen en route for Ballindalloch and Inverness – saw Milroy about Dee Salmon Fishing Improvement Association and their correspondence with Sir David Stewart, also Mr Mortimer who says he was not aware of the nature of the correspondence. We resolved not to trouble Sir D Stewart at present as matters are now settled for another year by Mr Garrow having taken the fishing opposite Sir David's water and it would be useless to acquire the one without the other.*

1907

Wednesday 29 May: *Drove to the Danzig to fish with Donald Stewart & Arthur Grant. The former landed one salmon, I landed 3, Arthur who took the last chance had no luck. Got back at 4 pm & attended to business.*

1909

Thursday 11 February: *Dee Salmon Fishings opened today. Tried the water from Corbiehall* [now more commonly known as Corbie's Haugh on the Abergeldie beat] *to Pool Sleck* [now more commonly known as Polslake on the Abergeldie beat] *and landed 3 clean salmon of weights 6, 8, 8 lbs. Polmahalmick* [Pol Mahalmick on the Abergeldie beat] *2, Dalraddie Stream* [on the Abergeldie beat, its name meaning 'field of the little road'] *1. Landed a kelt in Pool Sleck. Had a fish on first of all in Corbiehall Pool at 10.30 am but lost him. Then landed first clean fish from Polmahalmick at 12 noon, 2nd fish Dalraddie Stream one o'clock, 6 lbs. Kelt at Pool Sleck 1.30 o'clock, 3rd clean fish 8 lbs Polmahalmick 2 o'clock. River rather small with ripple from east & ice forming in rod rings. Froth from distillery passing down all the time. Only one other fish got by John Laird. Keepers all trying it.*

Wednesday 7 April: *Met Mr W.L. Calderwood* [a prolific author of fishing books], *Fishery Board Inspector by appointment and had some discussion on salmon fishings on the Dee.*

Friday 4 June: *Saw Captain Ellison to whom the King has given permission to fish. Captain Ellison caught 4 salmon today.*

Saturday 5 June: *Cycled to Ballater to transact some banking business, going by Birkhall on my way back. Afternoon drove to above Inver and met Dr. Cluckie & David who were fishing there. They had (David) got one fish. I landed two, or rather hooked two which Dr C. landed. Weather fine.*

1911

Saturday 25 February: *Fished from 2.30 p.m. being the second time I have tried this season. Caught a small fish of 5½ lbs in the tail of Corbiehall Pool with an old favourite fly tied by myself the Dragon. Weather cold but free of snow.*

Saturday 1 April: *Busy in office till motor time when I went by car to attend the late Mrs. Saunders funeral. Fished in the evening & caught 2 salmon. Very pleasant mild day.*

Friday 21 April: *Mild weather. Had a cast in the evening & got 7 fish.*

1915

Thursday 11 February: *Spent night at Palace Hotel and came on by 8.5 am train to meet Arthur Grant at Polhollick where tried fishing, this being the opening day. No fish got above Long Pool* [a pool on the Birkhall beat of the River Dee] *at Glenmuick Manse which is reported Sturton, gillie, landed one from North side. Several inches of snow still on ground.*

Saturday 22 May: *Sir Charles Fitzwilliam who started fishing HM water from Fife Hotel on Tuesday has now got five fish, having landed two of them today. Killed my 1st fish (6 lbs) of the season on lowest Clachanturn pool at 9 pm with middle sized "dragon."*

Saturday 12 June: *Had a cast in the evening at Clachanturn and landed a fish of 15½ lbs, in fact nearly 16 lbs, hooked by the lip with a small Green Charm double iron and very fine gut. Got no further rises. Weather hard and clear.*

Blue Charm

The Blue Charm (Figure 2.8) is one of the most famous low-water flies, yet none of the compilers of Salmon fly pattern books gets its 'inventor' right: Kelson attributed it to William Brown and, like sheep, everyone followed.

Murdoch first lists the pattern in the *Fishing Gazette* on 14th June 1884, stating that:

> The Blue Charm is as good a grilse fly as can be used from Banchory to Ballater; indeed, as its name implies, it is a perfect charmer. During the day nothing proves more effective in a moderately sized water, or a fairly heavy water not too much discoloured. When this fly takes well in the day time a small Jock Scott may be relied on in the evening. With no purely grilse fly we know of is the angler so little dependant on shade.'

Murdoch also states that the Blue Charm is 'one of a well known Deeside keeper'. In 1888, he reveals this well-known Deeside keeper: 'It [the Blue Charm] is one of the inventions of Frank Farquharson, fisherman, Blackhall, who is a real "good-sport" and a first rate rod, with no end of experience of the best reaches of the river.' This is the first published dressing:

Tag: Silver thread.
Tail: Small topping.
Butt: Black herl.
Body: Black silk floss.
Ribbed: Narrow silver tinsel, 5 turns.
Wings: Strips of mallard; very narrow strip distinctly marked teal over centre with mallard on either side, topping all over.
Hackle: Bright blue hackle halfway down body.
Head: Black.
Nos. 6 and 7 are very suitable sizes.

In May 1891, Murdoch again published a pattern for the Blue Charm, this time with some small but significant changes. He also makes the observation of 'An all-round killer – especially good on clear evenings about and after sunset in clear water, and in brown water under a strong sun.' The main changes were to the ribbing, now silver flat worm, and the hackle, 'greenish blue – long and pretty full – at shoulder only'.

The Blue Charm is still in use on the River Dee, both with its traditional mallard wing and in its more modern form with a wing made from squirrel hair.

Green Charm

The Green Charm (Figure 3.15) is a rare variant of the famous Blue Charm pattern (Figure 2.8). It is mentioned in both William Garden's 1907 and 1917 catalogues, and also appears in William

ROAD AND RIVER LINN OF DEE.

Figure 3.15 Green Charm tied by Eddie Kublin

Brown's list of flies for 1902, but not in their 1897 catalogue; in addition, it was present in Playfair's 1920s list. The pattern details are listed in Frederick Hill's *Salmon Fishing: The Greased Line on Dee, Don and Earn* (1948).

Tag:	Flat silver tinsel.
Tail:	Topping.
Body:	Dark green silk with flat silver tinsel.
Hackle:	Pale green.
Wing:	Teal.

Tuesday 22 June: *Afternoon cycled as far as Garlin Pool to see Lord Annaly* [who held the role of Lord of the Bedchamber for the Prince of Wales between 1908 and 1910; when we meet him here, his position is Permanent Lord-in-Waiting to HM King George V] *who is fishing by The King's permission – He had got 1 salmon this morning and told me that he had landed 12 fish in all. His Lordship intends leaving tomorrow.*

The date of 22 June 1915 marks the end of any fishing references in John's diaries. John continued in his post at Balmoral until his retirement in 1919, when he moved to Kincairn House, a country house on the south bank of the Dee near Blairs, where he lived until his death in 1934.

To put John's own flies in context, I have highlighted, along with his flies, some of the standard flies that would have been in use on the Dee at the end of the 19th and start of the 20th century. I need to stress the word 'some' as this book did not set out to fully explore the complete history of the Dee fly; indeed, I have only scratched the surface of this fascinating subject. There are many more Dee patterns, a few of the more important ones being covered in the Appendix, which follows. I also hope to further explore some of the rare patterns such as the Aboyne Peacock, Ballater fly, Tilbouries, Nicol, Davie Caird, Wattie Plants, Saturday, Thunderer and Playfair's Favourite in future publications.

Appendix

William Brown's 1897 'Special list of salmon flies for the River Dee'

Aboyne Peacock[b] -/8	Eagle, Grey[d] -/8	Logie[c] -/8
Akroyd[b] -/8	Eagle, Yellow[d] -/8	March Brown[c] -/8
Badger[b] -/8	Fail-Me-Never[c] 1/3	Mar Lodge[a] 1/8
Ballater Fly[a] 1/6	Gardener[b] -/8	Minister of Drumoak[b] -/6
Balmoral[b] -/6	Gledwing[b] -/8	Nicol[b] -/8
Beaconsfield[a] 1/8	Glentanar[b] -/6	Rintoul[b] -/6
Blue Charm[c] -/8	Gordon[a] 1/8	Sailor[c] -/8
Bumbee[c] -/8	Jeannie[c] -/8	Saturday[a] 1/6
Cabbage[c] -/8	Jockie[c] -/8	Sherbrooke[a] 1/6
Clunie[c] -/8	Jonah[c] 1/3	Silver Blue[c] -/10
Colonel Keane[a] -/8	Kelly[c] -/8	Skier[b] -/8
Davie Caird[b] -/8	Killer[b] -/6	Tilbouries[b] 1/3
Druggist[a] 1/6	Lady Grace[b] -/6	Tricolour[b] -/8
Dunt[b] -/8	Lizzie[c] 1/6	

[a] Full dress Dee flies
[b] Dee-style strip wing flies
[c] Low-water or summer flies
[d] Eagles
[e] Note that the Minister of Drumoak is also known as the Dr Corbet

As mentioned earlier, William Brown, tackle-maker of Aberdeen, published this special list of flies suitable for the River Dee in his 1897 catalogue. I have reproduced it above, with the price (in shillings and pence) for a medium '2/0' sized fly. Price is generally a good indicator of the complexity of these flies. The higher the price, the more exotic the material and the more time the fly took to construct; as a benchmark, a 2/0 sized Jock Scott was priced at at 1/8, or one shilling and eight pence, and the most expensive flies listed are 2/- or two shillings. I have also indicated the categories into which each fly falls.

William Garden's 1907 list of plain flies: Dee patterns

The introduction to the salmon flies section of William Garden's 1907 catalogue reads:

> I take particular interest in, and give this department special attention, and it gives me great pleasure to know that my efforts to please my numerous customers, during the past forty years, have been remarkably successful. Long and practical experience, together with constant communication with customers throughout the United Kingdom and abroad, gives me exceptional opportunity to know what is required. No pains or expense being spared to turn out the very best work, the quality of the material and the excellence of the workmanship have gained for these flies a world-wide reputation.

The catalogue then has a 'General list of salmon flies,' a list of 'Fancy salmon flies, standard patterns,' a list of 'Plain flies, Dee patterns' and finally a list of 'Flies for use in low summer water.' Here I list the plain Dee patterns as a useful comparison to Brown's and Murdoch's lists.

Akroyd	Dunt	Killer White Wing
Balmoral	Glentana	Lady Caroline
Black and Tan	Golden Eagle	Lady Grace
Bumbee	Grey Eagle	Rintoul
Davie Caird	Killer Red Wing	

With the exception of the Bumbee and the Lady Caroline, these are all Dee strip wing or Eagle patterns

Brown Winged
Akroyd 6/0¾

White Winged
Akroyd 6/0½

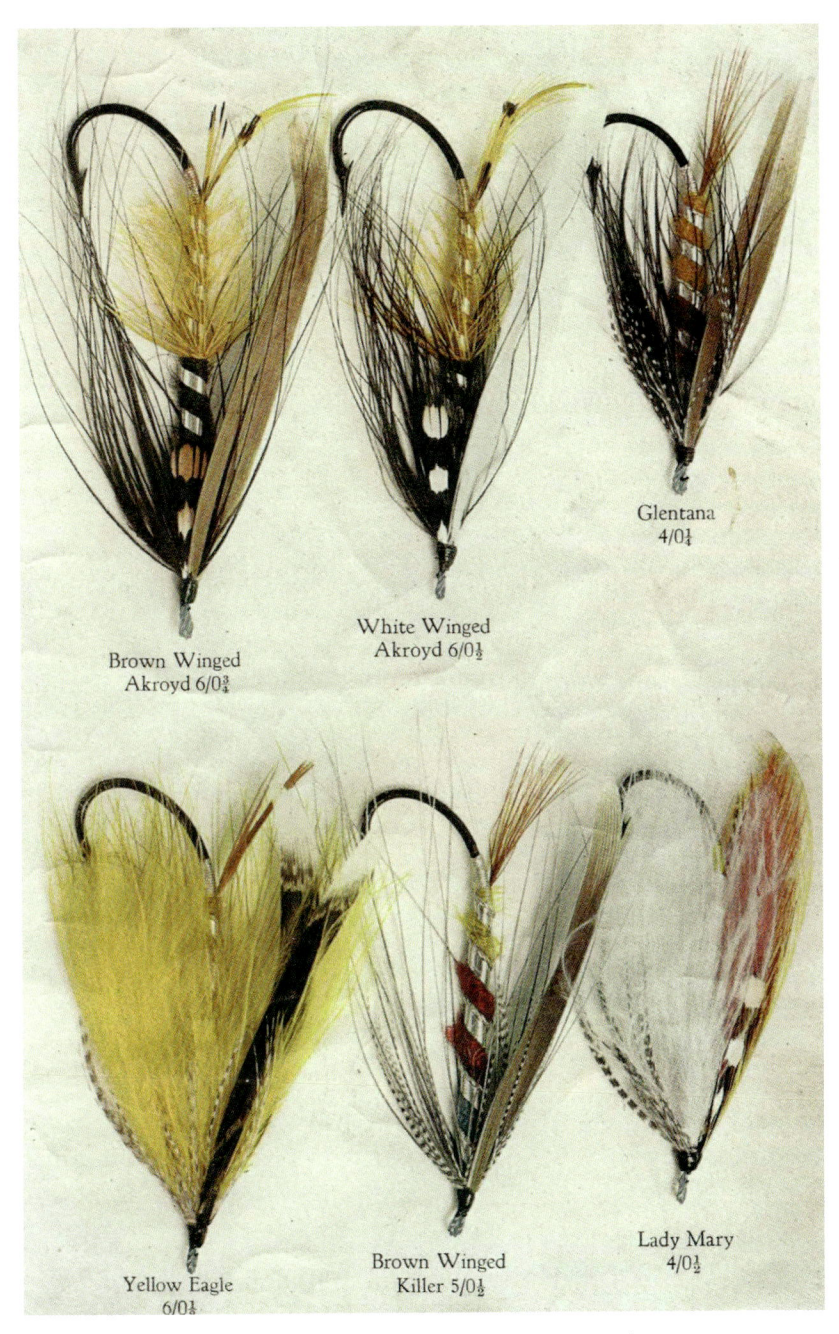

Glentana
4/0¼

Yellow Eagle
6/0¼

Brown Winged
Killer 5/0½

Lady Mary
4/0½

Figure A.1 A Dee fly plate from Garden's 1917 catalogue

Hardy's 1900 list of Dee flies

Hardy Brother's of Alnwick are one of the best known tackle-makers and publish comprehensive tackle catalogues; the following list is based on their 1900 edition. The catalogue has three lists of interest: 'The Best and most popular flies for the Dee,' 'Spring and Autumn Flies for the Dee' and 'Small summer flies for the Dee.' I have indicated the list(s) each fly fits into.

Akroyd [a,c]	Gordon [a]	Mar Lodge [a]
Black Doctor [a]	Green Highlander [a]	Poynder [a]
Blue Charm [b]	Green Peacock [b]	Sailor [b]
Bumbee [b]	Grey Eagle [a,c]	Silver Blue [b]
Butcher [a]	Hallidale Eagle [c]	Silver Doctor [a]
Dr Forbes [c]	Jeannie [b]	Thunder and Lightning [a]
Dunt [a,c]	Jockie [b]	Tricolours [c]
Dusty Miller [a]	Jock Scott [a]	Watson's Fancy [b]
Glentana [c]	Logie [b]	Yellow Eagle [a,c]

[a] 'The Best and most popular flies for the Dee'
[b] 'Small summer flies for the Dee'
[c] 'Spring and Autumn Flies for the Dee'

Murdoch's standard Dee strip wing patterns

In 1884, the Aberdeen-based correspondent for the *Fishing Gazette*, William Murdoch, conducted a survey into the most popular flies used on the River Dee during the spring season; in doing so, he created a list of 12 standard spring Dee flies (15 if you include the variants of the Akroyd, the Tricolour and the Killer). This article was published on 8th March, and the following is his introduction to the survey and the standard most popular flies that were identified:

With the kind co-operation of the local fishing tackle manufacturers and several well known and experienced Deeside anglers, we have, from a consensus of opinion expressed, been enabled to make a collection of twelve of the most popular mohair dressed turkey-winged flies used by anglers on the Dee during the spring fishing season; and further, to determine with accuracy, in the minutest detail, the particular dressing of each. Our Dee standard patterns, be it understood, are peculiar in respect that they are dressed with mohair instead of floss and have plain (turkey) instead of mixed wings. This style of dressing and make up has all along obtained and been regarded with high and general favour by anglers on Dee and Don. Though we can well perceive these flies to be of a special make, and particularly adapted for Aberdeenshire rivers, we have learned that they have been frequently used elsewhere with a gratifying amount of success. On account of their cheapness and killing effectiveness we have good reason for predicting that their popularity, as they become better known, will prove very much wider in its range in the future than hitherto. We speak advisedly because we have received ample evidence that they kill as well, if not better, as flies twice or three times their cost, while the loss entailed to the angler if they are destroyed or appropriated by a fish does not prove a distressing financial calamity. Though we ourselves have always had a predilection for fancy flies, we are honest enough to confess that our best results have been invariably obtained when using the strip wing lures. This remark applies exclusively to spring fishing, and if anglers attach any value to it they may regard it as being given with our best wishes for their success whenever they think of experimenting with any of our standard patterns.

The results of the survey concluded that the collection of 'standard' patterns for Dee spring fishing in 1884 comprises:

Akroyd	Glentanar	Rintoul
Balmoral	Grey Heron	Sir Peter
Dr Corbet [a]	Killer	Tartan
Gardener	Red-winged Heron	Tricolour

[a] Note: the Dr Corbet is also known as the Minister of Drumoak (and is listed as such in William Brown's 1897 list)

Most of these patterns have already been covered in the preceding chapters; however, Dr Corbet (or, in his *alter ego*, the Minister of Drumoak) and Sir Peter have been missed out, so not to offend them I have included the patterns here:

Dr Corbet

In his listing published in the *Fishing Gazette* on 1st March 1884, Murdoch states that "'Dr. Corbet,' or the 'Minister of Drumoak,' a favourite of long standing, is often used with good success in a moderate sized water during the spring season."

Tag: Silver tinsel.
Tail: Golden pheasant saddle feather.
Body: First half claret and green, second half claret.
Ribbing: Silver tinsel and gold twist.
Hackle: Grey heron; guinea fowl hackle down body.
Wing: Brown mottled wing with black tips.
Head: Black.

Sir Peter

When Murdoch published the pattern for Sir Peter on 1st March 1884, he noted that "'Sir Peter' is a very nice fly, not by any means new to the Dee, though the name may not sound familiar. We are to rank it amongst our standard patterns, because being a good killer, it is certain to obtain a wide popularity soon."

Tag:	Silver tinsel.
Tail:	Golden pheasant rump feather.
Body:	Mixture of orange and yellow mohair, mohair in the body well picked out.
Ribbing:	Silver tinsel with gold twist
Hackle:	Red cock hackle down body.
Shoulder:	Cock hackle (dyed claret).
Wings:	Mottled turkey of brownish tinge.
Head:	Black.

Two Dee strip wing flies not on Murdoch's list, which would have been included a few years later

The Dunt

I was surprised that the well-known Dee fly the Dunt (Figure A.2, A3 and A5) was not included in Murdoch's list of standard patterns. The first mention of the pattern that I could find was in the *Fishing Gazette* on 14th March 1885; perhaps this pattern was too new to make it onto the list published the year before. As it is such an iconic fly, it is probably worth looking at its history.

During the 1890s, the *Fishing Gazette* ran a series of articles called 'Famous Fishermen,' credited to 'MAC'. The article published on 1st March 1890 featured William Dawson:

> "A good man can't be a bad man too." He is a good man, and so was his father before him. "A capital fisher, a hardy chap, and a straightforward honest fellow," is the opinion of a brother fisherman of the subject of our present sketch, Mr. William Dawson, professional angler, Minonie, Bridge of Feugh, Banchory.

The article goes on to describe Dawson in great detail and glowing terms, even giving the reader an assessment of his physique: "Just now Dawson is at his best. In the full vigour of his manly prime, a

Figure A.2 Vintage Dunts

muscular, well-knit fellow, standing 5 ft 9½ in, dark, and with a keen eye and capital hands."

The final paragraph of the article is the important one in the history of this fly, giving both the story behind it and how it got its unusual name:

> Dawson is responsible for the invention of several flies. Seven years ago when he was fishing the Kineskie water [a beat on the River Dee] we used of an evening to drop down to see him work, and have a chat with him in piscine and piscatorial matters. When we got down to the river we used to call out to him from the top of the bank, "Have you got anything, Dawson?" and invariably his reply was, "O ti." "What did you get him with," we then queried, and he used jocularly to reply. "The proper dunt." This led us to invent a fly which we christened the "Dunt," to perpetuate Dawson's "Proper Dunt," which means the "proper thing." That the Dunt has proved the proper thing no one will deny. It is a particular favourite everywhere on the Dee, and in

one day more fish have been killed with it by one and the same rod than any other rod has got with any other fly in one day on the Dee within the last seven years – to wit, nine fish by Lord Strathallan on the Cambus O'May water some years ago in the spring.

If we take seven years away from 1890, we get the year of invention as 1883, so, as assumed at the start of this paragraph, the Dunt would have been a relatively new fly in 1884.

All the standard books containing salmon fly dressings after 1885 carry a dressing for the Dunt, each showing a little variation. Here I give the first published and in my opinion the prettiest pattern, from Murdoch's article 'Dee salmon flies for spring', published on 14th March 1885 (Figure A.3). The article carried a very good illustration of the Dunt (Figure A.4), emphasising its flat wing. It is interesting to note that Murdoch mentioned that 'Mr. George Smith, Tackle Merchant, Ballater, has a splendid stock of these patterns, most of which are proved killer on all reaches above, and a good many reaches below, that place.'

In the Lonsdale Library volume on *Salmon Fishing* by Eric Taverner, published in 1931, there is a good colour frontispiece plate of 'Orthodox Fly Patterns' that includes a fly called the 'Onset' tied by Hardy Brothers; the fly is obviously a 'Dunt.' This mistake is repeated in Taverner's 1947 volume *Fly Tying for Salmon*. The comprehensive list of salmon flies in JJ Hardy's authoritative 1919 book *Salmon Fishing* details the pattern for the Dunt but does not include the Onset, so I do not think this is a fault of Hardy's; more likely, it was Taverner's. It is, however, unfortunate, as this mistake has been repeated in quite a few of the modern fly pattern books, and the name was also incorrectly used by the famous Brora-based fly-tier Megan Boyd.

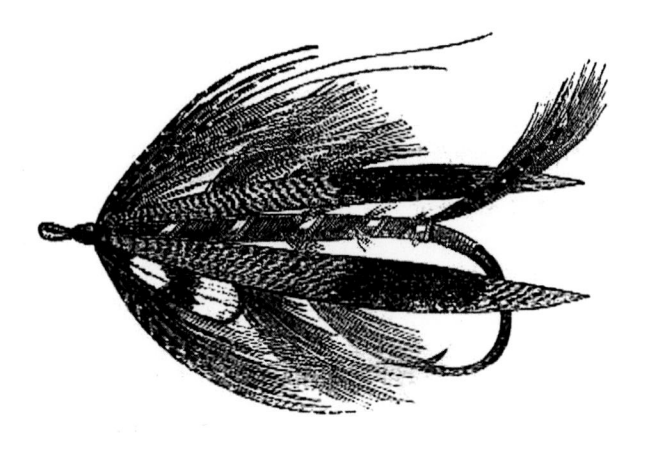

Figure A.3 An illustration of the Dunt from the *Fishing Gazette*, 1885

Tag: Silver thread and light blue floss.
Tail: A topping and spring of pintail.
Body: Orange shaded into fiery brown mohair – two fifths of the former, three fifths of the latter – fairly picked out.
Ribbed: Broad flat silver tinsel and gold twists, five turns.
Hackle: Black heron, over the fiery brown only, and so wound on as to give 20 to 25 fibres.
Shoulder: Teal, sparingly.
Wings: Brown turkey strips having a rich dark bar and white tip, with a sprig of teal between them on the top.
Cheeks: Jungle.
Head: Black.

Figure A.4 A spectacular vintage Moonshine

The Moonshine

One of my favourite Dee strip wing flies is the Moonshine (Figure A.4 and A.5), which is rare thing to find in its original vintage form. There has been a lot of confusion around this pattern, mostly started by Pryce-Tannatt in *How to Tie Salmon Flies* (1914) and then consistently incorrectly represented in modern books about salmon flies. As far as I am aware, there is no published dressing of the Moonshine in contemporary accounts. However, there is a very good illustration of it in a 1930s Forrest of Kelso catalogue plate of Dee flies (Figure A.5), and I also have some vintage examples in my fly collection; the one in Figure A.4 is a 9/0 beauty.

The first listing of the Moonshine that I have found is in a handwritten list of salmon flies offered for sale by the Aberdeen tackle firm of William Brown in 1902; it is not listed in Brown's 1897 catalogue, although it is listed in William Garden's catalogue of 1917 but not in his earlier 1907 edition. The confusion started when Pryce-Tannatt listed a fly called the 'Moonlight', which is simply a Moonshine with a different tail and tag:

Tail: A topping and a pair of jungle cock feathers (back to back).

Tag: Silver tinsel.

As this was a relatively new fly when Pryce-Tannatt was writing, it is impossible to tell whether this was a genuine mistake or whether he took an existing fly, tweaked the pattern and renamed it. To add further confusion, some modern compilers of salmon fly patterns have associated the Moonshine with the 'Moonlight on Mrs. Higginbotham,' which is a completely different, unrelated pattern for the Swedish River Em, documented by J D Greenway in his 1950 book *Fish, Fowls and Foreign Lands*. The original pattern for Moonshine is as follows:

Tag: Flat silver tinsel, yellow floss.
Tail: Topping, chatterer or kingfisher.
Butt: Black ostrich.
Body: 1/2 flat silver tinsel ribbed fine oval silver, veiled with blue chatterer or kingfisher above and below, butted black ostrich, 1/2 black floss ribbed broad flat silver tinsel.
Hackle: Black over floss.
Throat: Gallina.
Wing: Pale cinnamon turkey (although many vintage versions have white turkey).
Head: Black.

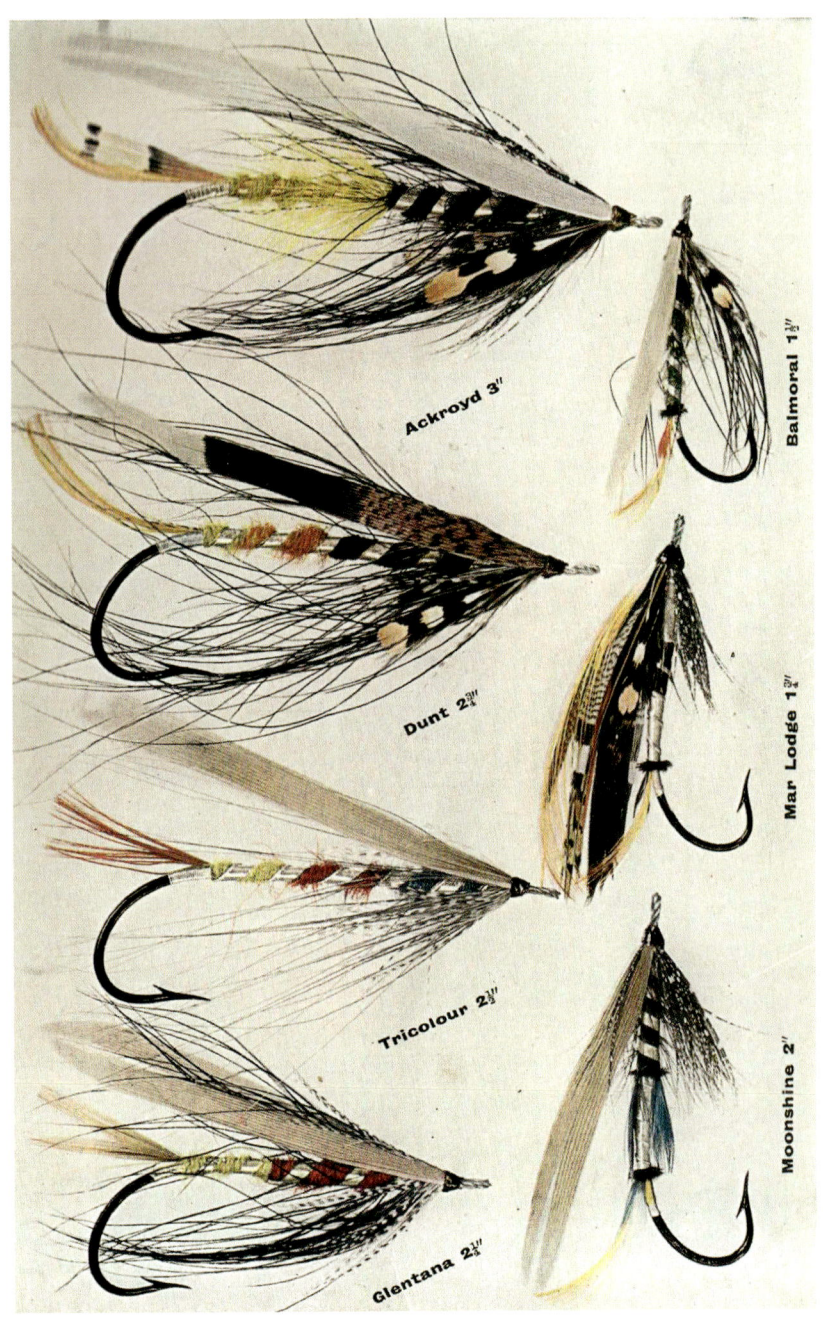

Figure A.5 Dee fly plate from Forrest of Kelso's catalogue of the 1930s

A comparison of beats on the River Dee, 1900–2015

The ownership and structure of the beats on the River Dee have changed since John Michie's day; the table below shows how they have changed over this period. I have also indicated who owned the beats in 1900. Note that details for the river above Balmoral are difficult to establish.

South bank of the Dee		North bank of the Dee	
1900	2015	1900	2015
Water of Dee (Duke of Fife) 10 miles	Mar Estate	Water of Dee (Duke of Fife) 10 miles	Mar Lodge
The Mar Water (Duke of Fife) 7 miles		The Mar Water (Duke of Fife) 7 miles	
Upper Invercauld (Mr A.H. Farquharson) 1.5 miles		Upper Invercauld (Mr A.H. Farquharson) 2 miles	
Lower Invercauld (Mr A.H. Farquharson) 1.5 miles		Lower Invercauld (Mr A.H. Farquharson) 1 mile	
Balmoral & Ballochbuie (Queen Victoria) 6 miles	Balmoral	Invercauld (let to Queen Victoria) 7 miles	Crathie
Abergeldie (Mr H. MacKay Gordon let to Queen Victoria) 6 miles	Abergeldie	Invercauld Water (Mr A.H. Farquharson) 9 miles	Lower Invercauld

South bank of the Dee		North bank of the Dee	
1900	2015	1900	2015
Birkhall (Queen Victoria) 2 miles	Birkhall	Morven Water (Mr J.M. Keiller) Less than a mile	Morven
Glenmuick or Pannanich (Sir Allen Mackenzie) 3 miles	Glebe Glenmuick	Monaltrie (Mr A.H. Farquharson) 5 miles	Monaltrie
Glen Tana (Sir W. Cuncliff Brooks) 7.5 miles	Headinch	Cambus O'May (Mr Barclay Harvey) 3 miles	Cambus O'May
	Dee Castle Waterside	Glen Tana (Sir W. Cuncliff Brooks) 4.5 miles	Dinnet Farrar
Glen Tana (let to Huntly Arms Hotel) 2 miles	Craigendinnie	Aboyne Castle (Marquis of Huntly) 4 miles	Aboyne Castle
Huntly Lodge (Mr J.R. Heaven) 3 miles	Birse	Huntly Arms Hotel 3 miles	Aboyne Red Brae Drumnagesk
		Upper Dess (Major D.F. Davidson) 1 mile	Upper Dess
Carlogie (Mr W.E. Nicol) 3 miles	Carlogie	Lower Dess (Major D.F. Davidson) 1 mile	Lower Dess
		Kincardine (Mrs Pickering) 2 miles	Kincardine

South bank of the Dee		North bank of the Dee	
1900	2015	1900	2015
Ballogie (Mr W.E. Nicol) 2.5 miles	Ballogie	Borrowstone (Mrs Pickering) 2.5 miles	Borrowstone
Commonty (Crown Property) 2 miles	Commonty	Sluie (Mr D. Davidson) O.25 mile	Sluie
Blackhall (Mr J.T. Hay) 5 miles	Upper Blackhall	Woodend (Sir T. Burnett) 2 miles	Woodend
	Middle Blackhall	Cairnton (Sir T. Burnett) 2 miles	Cairnton
	Little Blackhall	Inchmarlo (Mr D. Davidson) 1 mile	Inchmarlo Little Blackhall
	Lower Blackhall	Kineskie (Sir T. Burnett)	Kinneskie
Riverstone Under a mile	Banchory	Banchory Lodge Under a mile	Banchory
Inverey (Mr J.W.E. Douglass) 2 miles	Invery Knappach	Crathes (Sir T. Burnett) 5 miles	Invery Crathes
West Durris (Mr H.R. Baird) 3 miles	West Durris		Lower Crathes
Durris (Mr H.R. Baird) 3 miles	Durris	Park (Mr J. Penny) 3 miles	Park
Lower Durris (Mr H.R. Baird) 1.5 miles	Lower Durris	Park Water (Mr J. Penny) 0.25 mile	

South bank of the Dee		North bank of the Dee	
1900	2015	1900	2015
Tilbouries (Sir Cosmo Gordon) 1.5 miles	Tilbouries	Drum (Mrs Irvine) 4 miles	Upper Drum Drum
Altries (Mr A. Kinloch)	Alfred's Pot Altries	Culter (Mr. Duff)	Altries
Mary Culter (Sir Cosmo Gordon) 1.5 miles	Mary Culter Culter		Culter
Kingcausie (Mr A.J. Fortescue) 1.5 miles	Kingcausie	Kingcausie (Mr A.J. Fortescue) 1.5 miles	Kingcausie
Blair College 1 mile	Blairs	Blair College 1 mile	Blairs
Heathcot and Ardoe (Mr A.M. Ogston) 2.5 miles	Heathcot Ardoe	Murtle (Mr W. Dunn)	Murtle
Banchory Devenick (Sir D. Stewart) 2 miles	Banchory Devenick	Inchgarth (Mr W.R. Reid) 0.75 mile	Inchgarth
		Garthdee 1.5 miles	Banchory Devenick

Bibliography

While researching the material for this little book, I referred to the following books, catalogues and maps.

AKROYD, Charles H. *A Veteran Sportsman's Diary*. Robert Carruthers & Sons, Inverness, 1926.
  Useful for his comments on the 'Akroyd' fly.

BLACKER, William. *W. Blacker's Art of Angling*. Published by the author, 54 Dean Street, Soho, London; printed by Anderson and Bryce, Edinburgh, 1842 & subsequent editions.

BROWN, William. *Brown's Fishing Tackle Price List*. Fishing Tackle Catalogue, Aberdeen. No date (1897).

BUCKLAND, John & OGLESBY, Arthur. *A Guide to Salmon Flies*. Crowood Press, Ramsbury, Marlborough, 1990.
  One of the best modern books on the history and style of salmon flies; highly recommended.

CALLAHAN, Ken & MORGAN, Paul. *Hampton's Angling Bibliography: Fishing Books 1881-1949*. Coch-y-Bonddu Books, Machynlleth, 2008.

DICKIE, John Low. *Forty Years of Trout and Salmon Fishing*. Heath Cranton, London, 1921.
  If you can get over Dickie's slightly arrogant style, his very stern expression

in the frontispiece photograph and his use of the prawn, this one of the most interesting books about salmon fishing on the Dee in the early 1900s.

FORREST & Sons, Kelso-on-Tweed, Scotland. ***Price List of Fishing Rods and Tackle.*** No date (c1930s).
Very good colour plates of flies, including an excellent one of Dee flies.

FRANCIS, Francis. ***By Lake and River: An Angler's Rambles in the North of England and Scotland.*** The Field, London, 1874.

FRANCIS, Francis. ***A Book on Angling.*** Longmans Green & Co., London, 1867 & subsequent editions.

GARDEN, William. ***Descriptive Price List.*** Fishing Tackle Catalogue. No date (1907).

GARDEN, William. ***Descriptive Price List.*** Fishing Tackle Catalogue. No date (1917).
This edition has very good colour plates of flies, including four of salmon flies. The salmon fly plates include 'Typical Dee spring flies,' 'Standard patterns,' 'Flies for summer fishing' and 'Spey patterns.'

GREENWAY, J D. ***Fish, Fowl & Foreign Lands.*** Faber & Faber, London, 1950.

GRIMBLE, Augustus. ***The Salmon Rivers of Scotland.*** Kegan Paul & Co., London, 1899–1900.

HALE, Captain John Henry. ***How to Tie Salmon Flies.*** Sampson Low & Co., London, 1892.
The second edition of 1919 is more useful as it has more fly patterns.

HAMPTON, John Fitzgerald. ***Modern Angling Bibliography: Books published on angling, fisheries and fish culture from 1881 to 1945.*** Herbert Jenkins, London, 1947.

HARDY, John James. ***Salmon Fishing.*** Country Life and George Newnes, London, 1907.
Good for its 40-page appendix on salmon fly dressings (the list of flies is the same as in the second edition of Hale).

HILL, Frederick. *Salmon Fishing: The Greased Line on Dee, Don and Earn.* Chapman & Hall, London. 1948.
> *This gem of a book was written by the gillie of the Carlogie beat on the Dee, and includes some fly patterns not found elsewhere.*

HOULDSWORTH, Nigel. *Fisherman's Map of Salmon Pools on the River Dee.* No date.

INNES, Colin. *The Salmon Flies of James Harper, Proprietor of William Brown Fishing Tackle, Aberdeen, 1901-1945.* Coch-y-Bonddu Books, Machynlleth. 2017.
> *Another in the Angling Monograph series that was written after the first edition of* The Lost Salmon Flies of Balmoral *was published, this book explores the history of the Aberdeen fishing tackle firm of William Brown and documents the salmon patterns that James Harper listed between 1901 and 1945.*

KELSON, George Mortimer. *The Salmon Fly.* Privately published, 1895.

KELSON, George Mortimer. *The Land and Water Flies 1886–1902.* The Flyfisher's Classic Library, 1993.

LANIGAN-O'KEEFFE, Martin. *Farlows Salmon Flies: An illustrated catalogue of Farlows' pattern salmon flies 1870 to 1964.* Coch-y-Bonddu Books, Machynlleth. 2017.
> *An excellent book that documents and illustrates the reference collection of salmon flies built up by the London tackle firm of Charles Farlow between 1870 and 1964.*

MACKINTOSH, Alexander. *The Driffield Angler.* H. Mozley, Gainsborough, 1806.

MAXWELL, Sir Herbert Eustace. *Salmon and Sea Trout.* Lawrence & Bullen, London, 1898.

MARSTON, Robert Bright. *The Fishing Gazette.*
> *I used issues from 1880 to 1920 of this weekly publication.*

MURDOCH, William G Burn. ***More Light on the Salmon.*** The Fishing News, Aberdeen. No date (1925).
> *A great little book about salmon migrating from the North Sea to the source of the River Dee. It contains much information on beats, pools and flies that the fish encounter on their journey, but unfortunately not the fly patterns.*

PARKER, Maud. ***Fisherman's Map of Salmon Pools On the River Dee.*** John Bartholomew & Son Ltd., Edinburgh, 1933.

PLAYFAIR, Charles. ***Nett Price List of Rods, Flies, Casts, Tackles & Minnows.*** Fishing Tackle Catalogue, Aberdeen. No date (1920s).

PRYCE-TANNATT, Thomas Edwin. ***How to Tie Salmon Flies.*** A. & C. Black, London, 1914.

RUDD, Donald G Ferris ('Jock Scott'). ***Greased Line Fishing for Salmon.*** Seeley Service, London, 1935.

RUDD, Donald G Ferris ('Jock Scott'). ***Fine and Far Off: Salmon Fishing Methods in Practice.*** Seeley Service, London, 1952.

SMITH, Robert. ***A Queen's Country.*** John Donald, Edinburgh, 2000.
> *A very useful modern book that describes Balmoral and its environment through a series of walks. No fishing is mentioned, but it does have a good photograph of King George V hauling in the nets on Loch Muick (see Michie's diary entry for the 20th August 1892).*

TAVERNER, Eric. ***Salmon Fishing.*** Lonsdale Library, Seeley Service, London, 1931.

TAVERNER, Eric. ***Fly Tying for Salmon.*** Seeley Service, London, 1942.

TOLFREY, Frederic. ***Jones's Guide to Norway and Salmon-fisher's Pocket Companion.*** Longman, Brown, Green & Longman, London and J. Jones, 111 Jermyn Street, London, 1848.

WADE, Henry. *Halcyon, or Rod-fishing with Fly, Minnow and Worm to which is added a Short and Easy Method of Dressing Flies, With a Description of the materials.* Bell & Daldy, London, 1861.

WALBRAN, Francis Maximilian. *Walbran's British Angler, First Series.* Goodall & Suddick, Leeds/Simpkin, Marshall & Co, London. 1889.

> This often-overlooked book is important as it includes some of William Murdoch's fly patterns.